Meal Prep Cookbook for Beginners

Useful Weekly Plans

Simple, Healthy Keto Recipes

Ready-To-Go Meals for Kids and Busy Family

Easy Cooking Steps to Save Time, Money, Lose Weight and Feel Better

By Alan Dieter

Table of Contents

Breakfast: Avocado & Egg Breakfast

Lunch: Beef Soup

Dinner: Mediterranean Whitefish

Snack: Avocado Hummus Snack Jars

Breakfast: Broccoli Cheddar Egg Muffins

Lunch: Apples with Almonds & Figs Salad

Dinner: Pork Chops with Creamy Sauce

Snack: Bacon Cheddar Cheese Crisps

Introduction

Congratulations on purchasing your copy of the *Meal Prep Cookbook for Beginners,* and thank you for doing so. There is a wealth of information to get you started. We will discuss how to perform meal prep and better understand you are setting your unique methods using these suggestions. As you begin your nutritional journey, it's vital to understand better the healthy eating pyramid is simply an elaborate grocery list.

The food pyramid is a triangular diagram introduced initially in Sweden in 1974. The *Food Guide Pyramid* was developed in 1992 by the United States Department of Agriculture (USDA) to display food groups according to their values. The plan was updated to *My Plate* in 2011. The guidelines are divided into four categories comprised of these food items:

- Vegetables are 40%
- Grains are 30%
- Fruits are 10%
- Proteins are 20%

Know What Your Body Is Craving

To maintain a healthier body, you need to take care of its needs and know what it's craving. These are a few suggestions to consider:

Soda: You may have a calcium deficiency if all you want is the delicious taste of soda pop. Try eating, kale, broccoli, sesame seeds, mustard greens, or legumes to help remove the urge.

Sugary Foods: Several things can trigger the desire for sugar, but typically phosphorous, and tryptophan are the culprits. Have some chicken, beef, lamb, liver, cheese, cauliflower, or broccoli.

Chocolate: The carbon, magnesium, and chromium levels are beckoning a portion of spinach, nuts, and seeds, or some broccoli and cheese.

Salty Foods: It is possible that you may have a chloride deficiency. Enjoy a few olives, celery, tomatoes, or add some sea salt to your diet.

Cheese: You may be lacking the essential fatty acids deficiency. Help remedy the craving with some walnuts, ground flaxseeds, chia seeds, sesame seeds, flax oil, legumes, broccoli, kale, or mustard greens.

Fatty or Oily Foods: The levels of calcium and chloride need repair with a serving of spinach, broccoli, cheese, or fish.

You will have an array of meal plans to choose from consisting of simple preps, Keto diet preps, and kid-friendly preparation lists.

Chapter 1:
Meal Prep Principles

Save a Ton of Effort and Time: All it takes is a few tasty recipes and a little bit of your valuable time. In most of the cases, these recipes are geared towards a fast lifestyle and will be ready with just a few simple steps. After some time and practice, you will know which ones will be your favorites.

Use Your Freezer: Purchase meat when it's on sale and buy it in bulk. Freeze it for later. Assemble your meals in zipper-type bags and defrost when you want a quick and easy meal.

Mix & Match: If you have a busy lifestyle, purchase veggies and fruits pre-chopped and peeled and create an omelet or a stir-fry dinner. Use divided containers and prep into them.

Use Batch Cooking: Use a big pot on the stovetop or a slow cooker to prepare a batch of soup, chili, curry, or other delicious meals. By using sheet pan meals and dump dinners, you can save a ton of time and have a variety of meals.

By using these suggestions and the additional ones provided in your new cookbook, you will derive so many more benefits, including eating healthier, dropping a few unwanted pounds, and saving money since you will eliminate wasted food. It all comes down to your organization and multitasking skills. It can begin by choosing one strategy each week to improve your meal prepping skills.

Meal Prep – Storage & Reheating

Don't store hot food in the fridge: Keep your refrigerator set at an adequate temperature (below 40° Fahrenheit). If your refrigerator is warmer than this, it promotes the growth of bacteria. Any drastic temperature changes will cause condensation to form on the food items. You need to let your prepared food cool down in the open air - before putting it in a container and closing the lid. The increased moisture levels can open the door to bacteria growth.

Label the Containers: There are some other things you have to consider when freezing your meals. You should always label your container with the date that you put it in the freezer. You also need to double-check that your bottles, jars, or bags are each sealed tightly. If your containers aren't air-tight, your food will become freezer burnt and need to be trashed.

Meat Cooking – Internal Temps

- **Poultry** - should reach a minimum of 165° Fahrenheit.
- **Whole cuts of lamb, pork, and beef** - a minimum of 145° Fahrenheit.
- **Ground veal, pork, lamb, and beef** - a minimum of 160° Fahrenheit.

Correct Refrigerator Organization

Since you are taking the incentive to understand meal prep better, you also have to consider the proper storage of your valuable products. You have several compartments in the refrigerator to store your prepared foods. You must understand which foods store best in each location.

- ***Lower Shelves:*** This is generally the coldest section of the refrigerator, making it an ideal space for dairy, eggs, and raw meat. Your unit may have individual drawers for these items to ensure a consistent temperature.

- ***Top Shelves:*** Once you have prepared your meals or smoothies, it's recommended to place them on the upper shelves since these are items used most often. They also have the most consistent temperature settings.

- ***Sealed Drawers:*** Fruits and veggies should get stored in this space while avoiding the mixing of meat, fruits, and vegetables. Storing these foods together can create a risk of cross-contamination.

- ***Doors:*** Many refrigerators have a door to access frequently retrieved food items - available as pullout drawers without opening the main door. Non-perishable items such as drinks, some condiments, water, and other items that don't quickly spoil could be placed here.

- ***Top:*** Don't place bread or baked products on top of the refrigerator. The heat from the fridge could cause it to spoil more quickly.

Equip the Kitchen

A Good Set of Scales: Portion control is essential for baking bread. You want a scale that will accommodate your needs. Consider these options:

- ***Seek a Conversion Button:*** You need to know how to convert measurements into grams since not all recipes have them listed. The grams keep the system in complete harmony.

- ***Removable Plate:*** Keep the germs off of the scale by removing the plate. Be sure it will come off to eliminate the bacterial buildup.

- ***The Tare Function:*** When you set a bowl on the scale, the feature will allow you to reset the weight back to zero (0).

Accurate Measuring Tools: A measuring cup and spoon system that shows both the Metric and US standards of weight is essential, so there is no confusion during food prep.

Sifter: Purchase a good sifter for under $10, and you will be ensured a more accurate measurement for your baking needs.

Immersion or Regular Blender & Food Processor: These are useful in many stages of meal preparation at the restaurant level as well as in your kitchen.

Buy a Spiralizer or a Sharp Knife & Paring Knife: You can prepare zoodles, which are noodles cut from zucchini easily.

Preparation – Useful Items

An unglazed terra cotta tile at the bottom of a clean oven or a baking stone might be a good investment if you are planning on doing a lot of baking at home. You can also purchase an upgraded stand mixer with a dough hook. It's a good idea to have a few different sized loaf pans.

You should also invest in several mixing bowls to use.

A bench knife, better known as a dough scraper, can be used to clean surfaces, divide the dough, and to pre-shape the loaves of bread. Some even use it to dice veggies and apples.

- *Sheet Pans/Rimmed Baking Sheets:* (2) 12x18-inch pans.
- *Skillets:* Choose from a cast-iron skillet or a 10-12-inch nonstick skillet with a lid.

- **4-Quart Saucepan:** Prepare veggies using this type of pan, for example.

- 8-quart covered stockpot: Prepare your favorite stews and soups.

- **Meat Thermometer:** To ensure proper cooking.
- **Garlic Press or Spice mill:** These two utensils add additional flavor to your food and reduce the temptation of using a shaker of salt.

- **Vegetable Steamer:** This is essential because it will make the preparation of healthy vegetables much simpler without the use of oil or butter.

- **Cutting Boards:** Purchase individual boards for produce and meat/fish/poultry. You can also purchase plastic cutting 'boards' which are easily cleaned

These are a few additional items that will assist you with the baking process:

- Measuring cups for liquid and dry ingredients
- Measuring spoons
- Rolling pin
- Medium to large-sized saucepan
- Rubber spatula
- Wire cooling rack
- Bread cutting board
- Electric mixer
- Plastic wrap – damp tea towel

- Parchment paper will be used for most of the recipes. The baking pans are lined with the paper, and the baked goods do not stick. For most baking needs, you can omit the oils if you choose the paper instead. However, some recipes use paper and oils.

Purchase or Prepare the Containers You Want to Use

These are some guidelines for those:

- Mason Jars – Pint or quart-sized
- Ziploc-type freezer bags
- Rubbermaid Stackable - Glad Containers
  - Freezer Safe
  - Microwavable
  - BPA Free
  - Reusable
  - Stackable

Popsicle Molds or Push-Up Pop for Smoothies

You can purchase ice-pop clear pouches for <u>one-time</u> use or use a mold to reuse many times. Save money by using freezer bags to avoid using freezer space with a quart-sized freezer-safe Mason jar.

Chapter 2: Multitasking Skills Using Time Organization

Meal prep might seem a bit challenging at first, but remember—you don't need to prep all of your meals at one time. You can begin with the meats one evening, and veggies the next; it's all up to you!

- **Time Selection:** Choose a time to do your meal prep, so you do not have any interruptions

- ***Take Advantage of Your Crockpot & Slow Cooker:***
  You will find the crockpot a must if you have a busy
  lifestyle. These are just a couple of ways you can benefit
  from its use:

- ***Get Ahead of the Meal:*** Preparing food with a slow
  cooker can put you ahead of the game. You can prepare the
  cooker the night before if you have a busy day planned. All
  it takes is a few minutes of preparation. Just add all of the
  fixings into the pot and place it in the fridge—overnight.
  The next morning, transfer to the counter to become room
  temperature. Turn it on as you head out of the house.

- ***Take A Physical Inventory of the Pantry and
  Other Food Storage Areas:***
  Purchase your food items in bulk to save money.
  Therefore, you are saving money while on the ketogenic
  diet is vital. Purchasing your items in bulk can make a
  severe impact. Shop around and explore your areas for
  stores such as Walmart, Costco, or Sam's Club. These
  stores generally have bargain prices. Check your area for
  local farms that raise their animals on pasture feeding or a
  local market for fresh produce. After you find a good deal,
  stock up and purchase pantry items such as seasonings
  and flour. You can freeze many things and save a bundle of
  cash.

- ***Choose the Menu Plan:*** Gather your favorite recipes or
  try some new ones.

- ***Decide How to Prep:*** Do you want to prepare all of the
  chicken, pork, or other meal selections one night and the

veggies the next night? Or: Do you want to cook each meal individually but in bulk? No worries, either way, since each of the recipes has instructions for individual prep tips as well.

Consider These Additional Tips

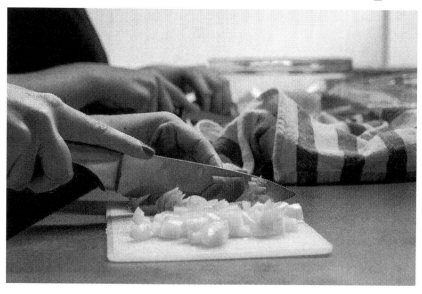

- Chop your veggies in advance. Make veggie packs to use for tacos, pasta, and stir-fries. You can also use them for snacks.

- Prep starches in advance, including rice and quinoa on a Sunday, and use them for the week.

- Prepare and freeze plenty of healthy fruits and yogurt into a delicious smoothie for the entire week. Enjoy one for breakfast or any time you have the craving.

- Purchase foods in bulk to be used for taco meats, breakfast burritos, fajita fillings, soups, egg muffins, and so much more.

- As you prep, include lean proteins for the weekends in a container for a quick grab 'n' go snack or luncheon for a weekend journey.

- See where your recipe ingredients overlap for different meals. For example, onions and peppers are often used.

- Prepare and freeze the freshly prepared chicken in different marinades so you can have a quick and healthy meal option.

- Consider freezing your meals even if it is just one portion, for those emergencies when nothing else will do!

- Prepare a batch of breakfast options ahead of time. Think about some of the recipes included in your new cookbook, such as overnight oatmeal in a jar if you are on-the-go.

- Prepare batches of dressings and sauces ahead of time, so you always have a delicious option to spice up your meals.

Guidelines for Dairy – Meats & Veggies

- ***Choose fresh meats and dairy when possible:*** Try to find meat and dairy that has an expiration date for as far in the future as possible. These choices will tend to remain fresh and last longer. This also applies to the "sell by" dates. The further in the future, either of these dates is, the surer you can bet that the food is going to last the week.

- ***Purchase Whole – Not Chopped Meats & Veggies:*** You can save big by chopping or slicing your own meats and vegetables. You will pay for the person that is doing the cutting for your convenience.

- ***How to Freeze & Reheat Your Meats:*** For meals that are scheduled to be eaten at least three days after cooking, freezing is a great option. Freezing food is safe and convenient, but it doesn't work for every type of meal. You can also freeze the ingredients for a slow cooker meal, and then dump out the container into the slow cooker and leave it there. This saves a lot of time and means you can pre-prep meals up to 1-2 months in advance.

The last food safety consideration you need to make with regards to meal prepping is how you reheat food. Most people opt to microwave their meals for warming, but you can use any other conventional heating source in your kitchen as well. The reason people love the microwave for heating their meal prep meals is that it's quick and convenient.

However, you have to be careful with microwaving because over-cooking can cause food to taste bad. To combat this, cook your food in one-minute intervals and check on it between each minute. You can also help your food cook more evenly and quickly out keeping your meat cut into small pieces when you cook it. You should never put food directly from the freezer into the microwave. Let your frozen food thaw first.

Food reheating and prep safety will become second nature over time. Meal prep can be overwhelming and require a lot of thought and patience, but it becomes a lot easier once you get used to it. Many of the mistakes are easy to avoid.

However, mistakes do happen, and as such, it's best to cook for short periods rather than longer ones, so you have less of a risk of making a mistake and needing to scrap everything you have prepared for that substantial period of time. While it is a lot and seems complicated, meal prepping is the best way to set yourself up for success.

Chapter 3:
Simple Meal Prep

Week 1

Day 1

Breakfast: Avocado & Egg Breakfast

Yields Provided: 4

Ingredients for Prep:

- Brown rice (.5 cup)
- Large eggs (6)
- Olive oil (2 tbsp.)
- Minced garlic (2 cloves)
- Chopped kale (4 cups)
- Freshly grated parmesan (.25 cup)
- Sliced avocado (1)

Method of Prep:

1. Prepare a pot of boiling water (1 cup) and prepare the rice of choice according to the directions provided.
2. Arrange the eggs in another pan with 1-inch of cold water. Once it's boiling, let it simmer for one minute. Cover and transfer the pan from the burner to rest for 8 to 10 minutes. Use a colander to drain the eggs and peel.
3. Use the medium heat setting to warm the oil. Toss in the pepper flakes and garlic. Sauté for one to two minutes. Fold in the kale, stirring until wilted (5-6 min.)
4. Shake in the parmesan.

Tips for Meal Prep:
1. Let the fixings cool thoroughly.
2. Use a divided container to store the eggs, rice, kale, and avocado.

Lunch: Beef Soup

Yields Provided: 4

Ingredients for Prep:

- Ground beef sirloin (1 lb.)
- Olive oil (1 tbsp.)
- Low-sodium beef stock (32 oz.)
- Whole wheat flour (.33 cup)
- Yellow onion (1)
- Mixed celery & carrots (1 lb.)

Method of Prep:

1. Prepare a soup pot using the oil (med-high heat setting) until it's hot.
2. Add the beef and flour. Simmer for about 5 minutes.
3. Chop and toss in the celery, carrots, and onions. Pour in the stock and stir. Lower the heat setting to medium.
4. Continue cooking the soup for about 15 minutes.

Tips for Meal Prep:
1. Cool thoroughly before ladling into four mugs or other storage containers.
2. Securely close the tops if using a plastic container.
3. Freeze for longer storage. Date the package and use it within several months.

Dinner: Mediterranean Whitefish

Yields Provided: 4

Ingredients for Prep:

- Raw white fish fillets - cod, tilapia, sole, etc. (4 - 4 oz.)
- Olive oil (4 tsp.)
- Mediterranean spice mix or chopped fresh oregano
- Optional: Fresh lemon (as desired)

Mediterranean Spice Mix:

- Dried onion flakes (4 tsp.)
- Dried oregano (1 tsp.)
- Crushed dried parsley (4 tbsp.)
- Ground thyme (1 tsp.)
- Crushed dried basil (2 tsp.)
- Garlic powder (1 tsp.)
- Sea salt (1 tsp.)
- Ground black pepper (.25 tsp.)

Method of Prep:

1. Warm the oven broiler to high.
2. Drizzle the fish with oil. Season using the Mediterranean spice mix.
3. Broil the fish until it's opaque and flakes easily when tested with a fork (3-5 min.).

Tips for Meal Prep:

1. Arrange the cooked fish in a shallow pan or baking sheet and pop into the freezer for quick freezing.
2. Wrap the fish in a moisture-resistant paper or freezer bag. It will store well for up to one month.
3. To thaw, just pop the bag into a pot of boiling water for about five minutes.

4. Spritz to your liking using fresh lemon juice before serving.

Snack: Avocado Hummus Snack Jars

Yields Provided: 4 jars

Ingredients for Prep:

- Chickpeas (1 can)
- Tahini (.5 cup)
- Avocado (1)
- Garlic (2 cloves)
- Lemon juice (1 tbsp.)
- Salt (.5 tsp.)
- Water (.25 cup)
- *Optional Fixings*:
- Sliced sun-dried tomatoes or antipasto
- Celery, carrot, or cucumber sticks
- Assorted chips, crackers, etc.
- Suggested: Vitamix
- Also needed: 4 salad mason jars/other containers

Method of Prep:

1. Rinse and drain the chickpeas. Mince the cloves and dice the avocado.
2. Combine all of the fixings (omit the optional fixings).
3. Remove the lid and stir as needed until fully mixed (5 min.)
4. Scoop the mixture into the jars and top with the desired toppings.

Tips for Meal Prep:
1. Store in the fridge for a quick and healthy snack.
2. Enjoy within the first two or three days for the best results.

Day 2

Breakfast: Broccoli Cheddar Egg Muffins

Yields Provided: 6

Ingredients for Prep:

- Whole eggs (8)
- Egg whites (4)
- Optional: Dijon mustard (.5 tbsp.)
- Broccoli (2 cups **)
- Shredded cheddar cheese (.75 cups)
- Pepper and salt (as desired)
- Diced green onions (2)

Method of Prep:

1. Set the oven at 350° Fahrenheit.
2. Prepare six muffin tins with paper liners or cooking spray.
3. Whisk all of the eggs, salt, pepper, and mustard. Blend in the green onions, broccoli, and cheese.
4. Divide the batter into the tins and bake for 12-14 minutes.
5. ** Use either fresh and steamed or defrosted and frozen broccoli.

Tips for Meal Prep:

1. Transfer the muffins to the countertop to cool.
2. Store in the fridge to use for a quick breakfast.
3. Serve when they are puffy and thoroughly cooked.

Lunch: Apples with Almonds & Figs Salad

Yields Provided: 6

Ingredients for Prep:

- Dried figs (6)
- Large red apples (2)
- Celery (2 ribs)
- Fat-free lemon yogurt (.5 cup)
- Slivered almonds (2 tbsp.)
- Carrots (2)

Method of Prep:

1. Chop the figs and celery. Peel and grate the carrots. Core and dice the apples.
2. Mix the fixings, beginning with the celery, apples, and figs.
3. Prep the carrots and almonds and store them in individual dishes if desired.

Tips for Meal Prep:

1. Store the fixings in the fridge using either individual salad dishes or in one large bowl. Be sure the salad is covered.
2. Stir and blend in the yogurt when it's mealtime.
3. Garnish with the carrots and almonds.

Dinner: Pork Chops with Creamy Sauce

Yields Provided: 4

Ingredients for Prep:

- Black pepper and salt (.5 tsp. each)
- Onion powder (.5 tsp.)
- Center-cut pork loin chops (4 - Approx. 4 oz. each)
- Non-fat Half & Half (.33 cup)
- Fat-free chicken stock (.33 cup)
- Dijon mustard (1.5 tbsp.)
- Dried thyme (A pinch)

Method of Prep:

1. Shake the salt, pepper, and onion powder over the chops.
2. Using the med-high heat setting on the stovetop, prepare a large skillet with cooking spray.
3. After the pan is heated, arrange the chops in it and fry for three to four minutes per side. The internal temperature should reach a minimum temperature on a meat thermometer of 145° Fahrenheit.

Tips for Meal Prep:

1. At this point, place the prepared chops in a container with a lid to cool.
2. Measure and add the chicken stock into the pan and deglaze the browned bits. Stir in the mustard and Half & Half.
3. Lower the temperature setting to medium and continue cooking for about 7 minutes. When the sauce has thickened, add the thyme.
4. Set the sauce aside to cool. Freeze if you won't be using the sauce within one day.
5. Wrap the chops well and store them in the fridge until time to eat. Serve with the sauce and your favorite side dish.

Snack: Bacon Cheddar Cheese Crisps

Yields Provided: 3

Ingredients for Prep:

- Cooked bacon (3 strips)
- Shredded cheddar cheese (1 cup)

Method of Prep:

1. Set the oven ahead of time to 350° Fahrenheit.
2. Prepare a baking tin with a sheet of parchment paper.
3. Pour about one tablespoon of the cheese onto the tray for each serving. Break the bacon to bits and add to the piles of cheese.
4. Bake for 5 to 8 minutes and let cool.

Tips for Meal Prep:

1. Blot the grease away with a paper towel.
2. Fully cool and store in a container in the refrigerator until the desired time to serve.

Day 3

Breakfast: Gluten-Free Roasted Grapes & Greek Yogurt Parfait

Yields Provided: 4

Ingredients for Prep:

- Seedless grapes (1.5 lb./4 cups)
- 2% plain Greek yogurt (2 cups
- Olive oil (1 tbsp.)
- Honey (4 tsp.)
- Chopped walnuts (.5 cup)

Method of Prep:

1. Warm the oven to reach 450° Fahrenheit and place the pan inside.
2. Discard the stems from the grapes and rinse them. Wipe using a towel and toss into a mixing container.
3. Wipe with a towel and put it in a bowl. Spritz with oil and toss to coat and bake for 20 to 23 minutes. They will look slightly shriveled. Stir about halfway through the cooking process.
4. Take the pan from the oven. Cool for five minutes.
5. Meanwhile, assemble the parfaits by adding the yogurt to the glass.
6. Once the grapes are cooled, garnish the yogurt with a teaspoon of honey, two tablespoons of the walnuts, and a portion of the grapes.

Tips for Meal Prep:

1. Prepare each of the four servings into individual dishes.
2. Keep the parfait in the refrigerator for up to three days.

Lunch: Tomato & Olive Salad

Yields Provided: 10

Ingredients for Prep:

- Cucumbers (5)
- Red or purple onion (half of 1)
- Green olives (2.25 oz. can/jar)
- Black olives (5 oz. can or jar)
- Tomatoes (5 large)
- Crumbled feta cheese (4 oz.)
- Red wine vinegar (.25 cup)

Method of Prep:

1. Chop the olives, cucumbers, and tomatoes. Crumble the feta.
2. Combine all of the fixings except the vinegar.

Tips for Meal Prep:

1. Store the dressing and salad fixings in individual containers.
2. Pop it into the fridge until it's time to eat.
3. Drizzle the dressing on top of the salad and serve.

Dinner: Chicken & Asparagus Pan Dinner

Yields Provided: 8

Ingredients for Prep:

- Chicken breasts (4 lbs.)
- Avocado oil (1 tbsp.)
- Trimmed asparagus (1 lb.)
- Sun-dried tomatoes -(4)
- Thick-cut bacon (4 slices)
- Salt (1 tsp.)
- Pepper (.25 tsp.)
- Provolone cheese (8 slices)
- Also Needed: 1 baking pan

Method of Prep:

1. Slice the chicken into 8 thin pieces. Chop the bacon and tomatoes into one-inch pieces.
2. Heat the oven to reach 400° Fahrenheit.
3. Add oil to the baking pan with the chicken and asparagus. Top it off with the tomatoes, bacon, pepper, and salt.
4. Bake until the chicken reaches 160° Fahrenheit internally - or about 25 minutes.
5. Toss in the asparagus and cheese.
6. Garnish with the bacon and tomatoes. Bake another three to four minutes until the cheese has melted.

Tips for Meal Prep:

1. Simply prepare the chicken and store it in the fridge for several days.
2. Place it into plastic bins or freezer bags until ready to use.
3. Prepare the asparagus when ready to eat and combine with the cheese. Garnish and serve.

Snack: Bacon Knots

Yields Provided: 4

Ingredients for Prep:

- Raw bacon (16 slices)
- Shredded parmesan (.25 cup)
- Minced garlic (4 cloves)
- Minced parsley (1 tbsp.)
- Pepper & Salt (to your liking)

Method of Prep:

1. Straighten one slice of bacon. Tie it into a knot.
2. Take another slice, and tie another knot around the first one. Continue until done.
3. Place the chain on a parchment-lined baking tin.
4. Warm up the oven to reach 400° Fahrenheit.
5. Sprinkle the bacon with the garlic and bake for 15 minutes.

Tips for Meal Prep:

1. When crispy, remove from the pan and chill in the refrigerator until mealtime.
2. When it's time to serve, heat the oven to 400° Fahrenheit. Sprinkle using the parsley and cheese.
3. Bake for one or two minutes until hot. Break apart and serve.

Day 4

Breakfast: Spinach Muffins

Yields Provided: 6

Ingredients for Prep:

- Nonfat milk (.5 cup)
- Eggs (6)
- Crumbled low-fat cheese (1 cup)
- Spinach (4 oz.)
- Chopped roasted red pepper (.5 cups)
- Chopped prosciutto (2 oz.)

Method of Prep:
1. Set the oven temperature at 350° Fahrenheit.
2. Combine the eggs, milk, spinach, cheese, prosciutto, and red peppers. Whisk well.
3. Lightly spritz a muffin tray with a cooking oil spray.
4. Dump the batter into the muffin tins and bake until browned (30 minutes).

Tips for Meal Prep:
1. Cool thoroughly on a wire rack.
2. Arrange in a plastic container or freeze to enjoy later.

Lunch: *Arugula Salad*

Yields Provided: 4

Ingredients for Prep:

- Arugula leaves (4 cups)
- Cherry tomatoes (1 cup)
- Pine nuts (.25 cup)
- Pepper & salt (as desired)
- Grated parmesan cheese (.25 cup)
- Large avocado (1 sliced)
- Rice vinegar (1 tbsp.)
- Olive/Grapeseed oil (2 tbsp.)

Method of Prep:

1. Rinse and dry the leaves of arugula.
2. Slice the cherry tomatoes into halves and grate the cheese.
3. Slice the avocado.

Tips for Meal Prep:

1. Combine the arugula, tomatoes, pine nuts, and cheese into four salad containers.
2. Either place the slices to the side in another container or a divided container for storage.
3. When it is time to serve, add the oil and vinegar with a shake of pepper and salt.

Dinner: Jalapeno Popper Burgers

Yields Provided: 4

Ingredients for Prep:

- Ground beef (1.33 lb.)
- Finely chopped jalapeno (1)
- Cream cheese - reduced-fat (2 tbsp.)
- Mustard (2 tsp.)
- Worcestershire sauce (2 tsp.)
- Shredded cheddar cheese (.5 cup)
- Kosher salt - divided (.5 tsp.)

Method of Prep:
1. Combine all of the burger fixings. Divide into six patties and wait about 10 minutes before cooking for the flavors to mix.
2. Grill to your liking (four to six min. per side suggested). If you prefer, use a frying pan, and cook for five to six minutes for each side.

Tips for Meal Prep:
1. Let the burgers thoroughly cool. Store in the fridge for about three days.
2. When ready to eat, warm the burgers and serve with the desired garnishes.
3. Freeze in plastic containers with other meal items (veggies) or freeze individually in freezer bags.
4. *Note*: You can also use ground turkey.

Snack: Peanut Butter Power Granola

Yields Provided: 12

Ingredients for Prep:

- Pecans (1.5 cups)
- Almonds (1.5 cups)
- Sunflower seeds (.25 cup)
- Almond flour or Shredded coconut (1 cup)
- Swerve sweetener (.33 cup)
- Vanilla whey protein powder (.33 cup)
- Butter (.25 cup)
- Peanut butter (.33 cup)
- Water (.25 cup)

Method of Prep:

1. Set the oven at 300° Fahrenheit.
2. Prepare a rimmed baking tin with a layer of parchment paper.
3. Process the almonds and pecans in a food processor and add to a large bowl.
4. Fold in the sunflower seeds, sweetener, shredded coconut, and protein powder.
5. Place the butter and peanut butter in the microwave to melt. Pour over the nut mixture. Toss lightly. Mix in the water.
6. Spread the mixture evenly onto the baking sheet.
7. Bake for 30 minutes. Stir about halfway through the cycle.

Tips for Meal Prep:

1. Cool before storing in an airtight container.
2. Serve anytime.

Day 5

Breakfast: Greek Yogurt Pancakes

Yields Provided: 14 (5-inch pancakes)

Ingredients for Prep:

- Nonfat plain Greek yogurt (2 cups)
- Baking soda (2 tsp.)
- All-purpose flour (1 cup)
- Slightly beaten eggs (4)
- Salt (1 tsp.)
- 1% Low-fat milk (.5 cup)
- Vanilla (1 tsp.)

Method of Prep:

1. Use an electric mixer stand and scoop the yogurt and remainder of the dry fixings into the mixing dish, blending until just incorporated.
2. Whisk the milk, vanilla, and eggs. Combine everything.
3. Prepare the batter in a griddle pan or sprayed skillet until golden. When the bubbles begin, it's time to flip. Serve and enjoy.

Tips for Meal Prep:

1. Prepare the pancakes and cool them completely.
2. Store in the fridge if you are using them within a day. Otherwise it's best to freeze them in closed containers or zipper-type freezer bags.
3. Begin by placing two pancakes on a microwave-safe plate. Microwave at 100% power or high power for 1 to 1.5 minutes or until warm, turning once.
4. Add butter and syrup, and breakfast is served!

Lunch: Tomato Soup

Yields Provided: 4

Ingredients for Prep:

- Olive oil (1 tbsp.)
- Onion (1)
- Garlic (3 cloves)
- Carrots (3)
- Roasted tomatoes (15 oz.)
- Tomato paste (1 tbsp.)
- Veggie stock (1 cup)
- Tomato sauce (15 oz.)
- Dried basil (1 tbsp.)
- Black pepper (1 pinch)
- Dried oregano (.25 tsp.)
- Coconut cream (3 oz.)

Method of Prep:

1. Chop the onion, garlic, and carrots.
2. Heat a soup pot using the medium temperature setting. Pour in the oil to heat until hot. Toss in the onion and garlic to sauté for about five minutes.
3. Pour in the tomato sauce, tomato paste, carrots, stock, tomatoes, basil, oregano, and black pepper.
4. Stir the fixings well and continue cooking for another 15 minutes.

Tips for Meal Prep:

1. Cool the soup and pour it into a large container until time to eat.
2. When it is time to eat, pour in the cream, and blend using an immersion blender.

3. Portion the tomato soup into serving bowls and serve.

Dinner: Turkey Sloppy Joes

Yields Provided: 4 -1 cup each

Ingredients for Prep:

- Raw ground 93% lean turkey breast (1 lb.)
- Olive oil (1 tsp.)
- Medium onion (1)
- Garlic (2 cloves)
- Medium red bell pepper (1)
- Sea salt (.5 tsp.)
- Ground black pepper (.25 tsp.)
- All-natural tomato sauce, no salt or sugar added (1 cup)
- Worcestershire sauce, gluten-free (1 tbsp.)
- Raw honey/Pure maple syrup (1 tbsp.)
- Hot pepper sauce (1.5 tsp.)
- Optional: Fresh parsley (to taste)

Method of Prep:

1. Warm the oil in a large frying pan using the medium heat temperature setting.

2. Chop and add the garlic, onion, and bell pepper. Sauté for about one minute and add to a medium bowl. Set aside in a mixing bowl.

3. Add the turkey, salt, and pepper to the skillet. Simmer using the medium temperature heat. Stir often until the turkey is no longer pink (8 to 10 minutes).

4. Mix in the onion mixture, tomato sauce, hot sauce, Worcestershire sauce, and maple syrup.

5. Lower the heat to med-low, stirring occasionally until the sauce has thickened (15 to 20 minutes).

Tips for Meal Prep:
1. They are good in the fridge for 3-4 days.
2. Cool the *Sloppy Joes* thoroughly in the fridge before you freeze them in labeled freezer bags. Lay them flat in your freezer, so you can stack the frozen meals for three to six months.
3. Chop and sprinkle each serving with parsley before serving.
4. Place on 1 piece of whole-wheat toast or romaine lettuce leaves.

Snack: Fried Queso Fresco

Yields Provided: 5

Ingredients for Prep:

- Coconut oil (1 tbsp.)
- Queso fresco (1 lb.)
- Olive oil (.5 tbsp.)

Method of Prep:
1. Chop the cheese into cubes.
2. Warm both of the oils to the smoking point, and toss in the cheese.
3. Fry the cheese, flipping once until well browned.
4. Remove and let the cheese rest to cool.

Tips for Meal Prep:
1. Drain on towels to remove the oil.
2. Store in a closed container to enjoy anytime.

Day 6

Breakfast: Omelet Waffles

Yields Provided: 2

Ingredients for Prep:

- Black pepper (1 pinch)
- Eggs (4)
- Low-fat shredded cheddar cheese (.25 cup)
- Chopped ham (2 tbsp.)
- Chopped parsley (2 tbsp.)

Method of Prep:
1. Warm and lightly grease a waffle iron with a spritz of the cooking oil spray.
2. Combine all the fixings in a mixing container.
3. Empty the mixture into the iron and cook for four to five minutes.

Tips for Meal Prep:
1. Cool the waffles entirely before freezing, so they don't collect ice in the freezer.
2. Place them on a cookie tin, so they do not touch and let them fully freeze. If you want to prepare more, stack the trays for a few hours.
3. Place into resealable freezer bags until needed.

Lunch: Chicken – Apple Spinach Salad

Yields Provided: 4

Ingredients for Prep:

- Onion (.5 cup)
- Spinach (4 cups)
- Chopped toasted pecans (.25 cup)
- Acai dressing or your favorite (.75 cup)
- Cooked breast of chicken (2 cups)
- Granny Smith apples (2 cups)

Method of Prep:

1. Prep the Fixings: Dice the chicken. Chop the apples, pecans, and spinach. Slice the onion.
2. Use individual containers or one large salad dish to prep the salad, beginning with a layer of spinach.
3. Arrange the remainder of the fixings.

Tips for Meal Prep:

1. Note: You can wait to slice the apple if desired.
2. Cover the prepared salad with a lid or a layer of plastic wrap until serving time.
3. Sprinkle with the dressing to serve.

Dinner: Apricot BARBECUE Chicken

Yields Provided: 6

Ingredients for Prep:

- Breasts of chicken (1 lb.)
- Sugar-free BARBECUE sauce (.5 cup)
- Sugar-free Apricot jam (.5 cup)
- Low-sodium soy sauce (2 tbsp.)
- Ground ginger (1 tsp.)
- Onion powder (1 tsp.)
- Garlic powder (1 tsp.)

Method of Prep:

1. Warm the oven temperature at 350⁰ Fahrenheit.
2. Trim away the skin and bones from the chicken. Prepare a baking sheet with foil and add the chicken.
3. Whisk the barbecue sauce, jam, seasonings, and soy sauce together in a mixing container. Pour over the chicken and bake for about 30 minutes.

Tips for Meal Prep:

1. This is a great choice for meal prep. Make this entire recipe and let it cool.
2. Store in the refrigerator for up to two days or freeze for later use.
3. Enjoy with your favorite side dishes.

Snack: Veggie Egg Cups

Yields Provided: 6 (2 each)

Ingredients for Prep:

- Homemade salsa (12 tbsp.)
- Green onions (2)
- Medium red bell pepper (1)
- Mushroom (1 cup)
- Large eggs (12)
- Nonstick cooking spray
- Sea salt and black pepper (as desired)

Homemade Salsa:

- Fresh cilantro (1 bunch)
- Small sweet onion (1)
- Garlic (3 cloves)
- Sea salt (.5 tsp.)
- Medium tomatoes (3)
- Medium jalapeno (1)

Method of Prep:

1. Prepare the salsa. Roast the jalapeno with the veins and seeds removed. Chop the cilantro with the stems removed. Finely chop and combine the jalapeno, tomatoes, garlic, onion, cilantro, and salt in a medium mixing container.
2. Prepare oven to 375° Fahrenheit. Spray a muffin tin with cooking spray.
3. Add the eggs, salt, and pepper in a large mixing bowl and whisk until blended. Finely chop and mix in the mushrooms, green onions, and bell peppers.
4. Fill each muffin cup evenly with the egg mixture.
5. Bake in the oven until a toothpick inserted into the center of the cups comes out clean (15-20 min.).

Tips for Meal Prep:
1. Freeze for Later: When completely cooled, put them in a gallon-sized freezer bag or container, squeeze out any air, seal, and freeze for up to 3 months.
2. Prepare from Frozen: Thaw overnight in refrigerator or pop into the microwave for a quick defrost.
3. To Serve: Top each egg cup with 1 teaspoon of homemade salsa

Day 7

Breakfast: Banana Oat Pancakes

Yields Provided: 8 (2 pancakes each serving)

Ingredients for Prep:

- Extra-virgin coconut oil (.5 tsp.)
- Old-fashioned rolled oats - dry (2 cups)
- Sea salt (1 dash)
- Ground cinnamon (.5 tsp.)
- Baking powder (1 tsp.)
- Large ripe banana (1)
- Large eggs (2)
- Unsweetened almond milk (1 cup)
- Pure vanilla extract (1 tsp.)
- Fresh mixed berries (3 cups)

Method of Prep:

1. Combine the almond milk, salt, baking powder, cinnamon, eggs, banana extract, and oats in a blender. Blend until it's creamy.
2. Pour the oil in a frying pan using the med-low heat setting.
3. Pour ¼ cup of batter into the skillet and cook for two to three minutes. The edges of the pancake will bubble when they're ready to flip. Cook for another 1.5 minutes.
4. Repeat the process until all of the batters are gone.

Tips for Meal Prep:

1. The pancakes that are not eaten can be frozen and reheated in a toaster.
2. Cool thoroughly, and place in freezer bags for longer storage.
3. When ready to eat, top with fresh mixed berries.

Lunch: Ham Salad

Yields Provided: 4

Ingredients for Prep:

- Mango chutney (1 tbsp.)
- Onion powder (2 tsp.)
- Light mayonnaise (2 tbsp.)
- Dried mustard (2 tsp.)
- Plain Greek yogurt - Nonfat (2 tbsp.)
- Cooked - chopped ham (1 cup)

Method of Prep:

1. Pulse the fixings (omit the ham or not) in a processor until creamy smooth.
2. Put the container in the fridge for 30-45 minutes or until needed.

Tips for Meal Prep:

1. For meal prep, place the salad into four individual bowls.
2. Leave in the refrigerator and enjoy on-the-run.

Dinner: Baked Chicken Fajita

Yields Provided: 4

Ingredients for Prep:

- Chicken breasts (1 lb.)
- Bell pepper (1)
- Onion (1 medium)
- Tomato (1 ripe)
- Cumin (1 tbsp.)
- Garlic powder (2 tsp.)
- Salt (1 tsp.)
- Black pepper (1 tsp.)
- Onion powder (1 tsp.)
- Chili powder (.5 tsp.)

Method of Prep:

1. Slice or chop the veggies. Slice the chicken into strips making sure to remove all of the skin and bone fragments.
2. Combine all of the seasonings in a mixing container and add the chicken. Toss.
3. Set the oven temperature at 375° Fahrenheit.
4. Use a misting of cooking spray on the casserole dish and add the prepared chicken in a single layer. Top with the veggies.
5. Bake 35-40 minutes.

Tips for Meal Prep:

1. This is yet another great option for meal prep.
2. Prepare as above and let it cool thoroughly.
3. You can put it into four separate containers for storage or freezing.
4. Enjoy with some salsa, cheese, on a tortilla, or any way you like it.

Snack: Mini Crustless Quiche

Yields Provided: 12

Ingredients for Prep:

- Large eggs (15)
- Plum tomatoes (3)
- Pepper jack cheese (.5 cup)
- Mozzarella cheese (1 cup)
- Sweet onion (.33 cup)
- Pickled jalapenos (.33 cup)
- Salami (1 cup)
- Heavy cream (.5 cup)
- Also Needed: Muffin tins - 11x15-inch

Method of Prep:

1. Warm up the temperature in the oven to 325° Fahrenheit.
2. Prep the veggies. Dice the tomatoes, onions, jalapenos, and salami. Shred the cheese.
3. Spritz the muffin tins lightly with a misting of cooking oil.
4. Whisk all of the fixings together and split the batter in the muffin tins.
5. Bake for 25 minutes.

Tips for Meal Prep:

1. Cool thoroughly and slice the quiche into 12 portions.
2. Wrap it in plastic wrap.
3. When ready to eat, microwave from frozen, using the high setting at 30-second intervals - probably no more than one minute.
4. If you don't slice it, cover it in foil. Place the prepared dish into an oven-proof container, and heat for 20 minutes using a 350° Fahrenheit oven.

Week 2

Day 8

Breakfast: Veggie Egg Scramble

Yields Provided: 6

Ingredients for Prep:

- Diced tomato (1)
- Large eggs (6)
- Baby spinach (3 cups)
- Minced garlic clove (1)
- Red or purple diced onion (half of 1)
- Freshly cracked black pepper and kosher salt (1 tsp. each)
- Olive oil (1.5 tbsp.)
- 2% sharp cheddar cheese - ex. Cabot (.5 cup)

Method of Prep:
1. Whisk the eggs, pepper, and salt.
2. Warm up the oil in a skillet. Toss in the spinach, onions, tomato, and garlic. Simmer until done or 5 to 7 minutes.
3. Pour in the eggs and simmer 3 to 4 minutes – stirring occasionally.
4. When set, let the container become room temperature and take it away from the burner.
5. Sprinkle the cheese. Serve and enjoy.

Tips for Meal Prep:
1. Prepare the eggs and set aside to cool.
2. Place in the fridge and take the fixings with you to work tomorrow for a healthy breakfast.

Lunch: Asparagus Soup

Yields Provided: 6

Ingredients for Prep:

- Cooked chicken breasts (2)
- Salt & black pepper (1 pinch each)
- Carrots (2)
- Chopped asparagus spears (12)
- Yellow onion (1)
- Spinach (4 cups)
- Minced garlic cloves (3)
- Low-sodium veggie stock (6 cups)
- Lime (half of 1)
- Olive oil (1 tbsp.)
- Chopped cilantro (1 handful)

Method of Prep:

1. Cook the chicken and remove the skin and bones. Finely chop the asparagus, yellow onion, and carrots. Mince the garlic cloves.
2. Use the medium heat setting on the stovetop, and add the oil to a soup pot.
3. When hot, toss in the onions and sauté for five minutes.
4. Next, toss in the garlic, asparagus, and carrots. Continue cooking for an additional five minutes.
5. Toss in the spinach with a dusting of the pepper and salt. Add the chicken and stock. Continue cooking for about 20 minutes.

Tips for Meal Prep:

1. Chill thoroughly before placing it in the fridge.

2. When it is time to eat, toss in the lime zest and cilantro.
3. Stir well and ladle the soup into serving dishes.

Dinner: Asian Glazed Chicken

Yields Provided: 4

Ingredients for Prep:

- Coconut aminos (.33 cup)
- Chicken thighs (8)
- Garlic (3 tbsp.)
- Balsamic vinegar (.5 cup)
- Olive oil (.25 cup)
- Black pepper (1 pinch)
- Garlic chili sauce (3 tbsp.)
- Green onion (1 tbsp.)

Method of Prep:
1. Set the oven temperature at 425° Fahrenheit.
2. Discard the bones and skin from the chicken. Mince the garlic and chop the green onion.
3. Prepare a baking sheet with a spritz of cooking oil spray.
4. Add oil to the pan along with the chicken, vinegar, aminos, chili sauce, onion, black pepper, and garlic.
5. Toss well and bake for 30 minutes.
6. When done, serve with the sauce.

Tips for Meal Prep:
1. This is super for meal prep since all you do is let it thoroughly cool.

2. Arrange the chicken into individual freezer bags or another type of storage container.
3. Be sure to label its contents and freeze.

Snack: Veggie Snack Pack

Ingredients for Prep:

- Foster Farms <u>Bold Bites Pouch</u>
- Cherry tomatoes (5)
- Red bell pepper (.25 of 1)
- Sugar snap peas (.33 cup)
- Baby carrots (.5 cup)
- English cucumber (.33 cup)
- Hummus (2 tbsp.)

Method of Prep:

1. Rinse all of the veggies.
2. Discard the seeds from the pepper and slice.
3. Slice the cucumber.
4. Measure out the rest of the fixings.

Tips for Meal Prep:

1. Fill a small reusable dipping sauce container with two tablespoons of hummus. Secure the lid and place it into the container.
2. Arrange the prepared vegetables into portions (bell peppers, cucumbers, tomatoes, carrots, and peas) and close the container.
3. Place in the fridge until you need a quick on-the-go snack. Serve with one package of *Bold Bites*.

Day 9

Breakfast: Spinach – Feta & Egg Breakfast Quesadillas

Yields Provided: 5

Ingredients for Prep:

- Olive oil (2 tsp.)
- Red bell pepper (1)
- Red onion (half of 1)
- Eggs (8)
- Milk (.25 cup)
- Black pepper and salt (.25 tsp. each)
- Spinach leaves (4 handfuls)
- Feta (.5 cup.)
- Mozzarella cheese (1.5 cups)
- Tortillas (5)

Method of Prep:

1. Warm the olive oil in a skillet using the medium temperature setting.
2. Dice the onion and peppers. Toss into the pan to sauté for 4-5 minutes.
3. Whisk the eggs, salt, pepper, and milk. Stir often and toss in with the onions and peppers until the eggs are done.
4. Fold the feta and spinach into the eggs, stirring until the spinach is wilted. Take the pan from the burner.
5. Spray another frying pan with a spritz of cooking oil and warm using the medium temperature setting. Add the tortilla and spread ½ cup of egg mixture on one side of the tortilla. Garnish with ⅓ cup of the mozzarella and fold over the tortilla. Cook until browned (2 min.).

6. Flip it and cook another minute. Continue until all are done. It should take no more than 25 minutes from start to finish.

Tips for Meal Prep:
1. Cool thoroughly on a rack and wrap in plastic or store in a resealable container.
2. Reheat on top of a paper towel in the microwave for 30 to 60 seconds.
3. Crisp on a grill or in a frying pan for two to three minutes.

Lunch: Salmon Vegetable Frittata

Yields Provided: 6

Ingredients for Prep:
- Eggs (6)
- Mushrooms (2 cups)
- Green onion (.25 cup)
- Butter or margarine (1 tbsp.)
- Smoked salmon (4 oz.)
- Skim milk (1 cup)
- Paprika (.25 tsp.)
- Pepper (.25 tsp.)
- *Also Needed*: Ovenproof skillet

Method of Prep:
1. Warm up the oven to reach 350° Fahrenheit.
2. Chop the onions and mushrooms. Sauté in melted butter in the pan for about three to five minutes.
3. Whisk the eggs with the milk, pepper, and paprika with a wire whisk until mixed.
4. Dice the salmon into small chunks. Fold into the egg mixture

with the cooked onions and mushrooms. Toss well.
5. Bake for 30 minutes.

Tips for Meal Prep:
1. Carefully transfer the pan to the stovetop to cool.
2. Slice into six wedges and store in the fridge.
3. *Option #1*: You can individually wrap the frittatas or leave them in the pan to enjoy for a full meal.
4. Option #2: Portion the frittata into sealed containers with your favorite veggies for another meal.
5. Freeze after the first or second day.

Dinner: Thai Peanut Chicken

Yields Provided: 6-8

Ingredients for Prep:

- Chicken thighs (2 lb.)
- Minced garlic (2 tsp.)
- Coconut milk (14 oz. can)
- Creamy peanut butter (.5 cup)
- Lime juice (3 tbsp.)
- Ginger (1 tbsp. - grated)
- Tamari or soy sauce (2 tbsp.)
- Honey (3 tbsp.)
- Toasted sesame oil (1 tbsp.)
- Garam masala (1 tsp.)
- Curry powder yellow (2 tsp.)
- Cumin (1 tsp.)
- Red pepper flakes (.5 tsp.)

Method of Prep:
1. Trim and discard the bones from the chicken.
2. This is a great prep recipe since you put it together and freeze it to pop into a slow cooker at a later date.

3. In a medium container, mix the coconut milk, lime juice, ginger tamari, honey, sesame oil, garlic, curry powder, cumin, garam masala, peanut butter, and red pepper flakes.
4. Whisk it all together until smooth. Add the chicken.
5. To Eat Now: Add the chicken and sauce to a crockpot and cook

Tips for Meal Prep:
1. Transfer chicken and sauce to a labeled container or freezer bag and freeze.
2. From thawed or freshly made, transfer the chicken and sauce into a slow cooker. Cook using the low setting for six hours or the high setting for four hours.

Snack: Beef & Cheddar Roll-Ups

Yields Provided: 1

Ingredients for Prep:
- Cheddar cheese (half of 1 slice)
- Thousand Island yogurt/Regular dressing (1 tbsp.)
- Tomatoes & onions (as desired)

Method of Prep:
1. Thinly slice and lay the roast beef onto a preparation surface.
2. Place the cheese, dressing, and veggies on top.
3. Roll it up and secure with toothpicks.

Tips for Meal Prep:
1. When you are ready to eat, cut them into halves.

Day 10

Breakfast: Breakfast Bowls

Yields Provided: 6

Ingredients for Prep:

- Yukon gold potatoes (2 lb.)
- Green pepper (1)
- Onion (1)
- Olive oil
- Seasoned salt
- Eggs (12)
- Freshly shredded cheddar cheese (4 oz.)
- Green onions (3)
- Optional Toppings: Salsa - tortilla & avocado
- Individual-sized glass containers with lids or Tupperware type (6)

Method of Prep:

1. Dice the cucumber, onions, and potatoes into 1-inch cubes. Deseed and chop the green peppers.
2. Warm the oven at 425° Fahrenheit.
3. Prepare a baking tray with a drizzle of oil and add the onions, potatoes, and peppers. Dust with the pepper and seasoned salt.
4. Split the veggies onto two baking trays and roast for 30-40 minutes. Rotate and toss the potatoes about halfway through the baking cycle.
5. Whisk the eggs pepper and salt until smooth.
6. Prepare a skillet using the medium temperature setting with a spritz of cooking oil. Lower the heat to the low-temperature setting, cooking until the eggs until barely incorporated.

Tips for Meal Prep:

1. Divide the fixings evenly into two containers. Cool thoroughly and sprinkle with green onions and cheese. Place a lid on each container.
2. Eat the meal within three days or freeze.
3. When ready to reheat from frozen, set the microwave at 50% power, and set the timer for 1.5 minutes. Stir until fully heated. Top to your liking.

Lunch: Chili Con Carne

Yields Provided: 12

Ingredients for Prep:

- Ground chuck (5 lb.)
- Large onion (1)
- Green and red bell pepper (1 each)
- Garlic cloves (2)
- Chili powder (.5 cup)
- Cumin (2 tbsp.)
- Chipotle (1 tsp.)
- Pinto/kidney beans (2 - 15 oz. cans)
- Tomato paste (10 oz. can)
- Tomato sauce (2 - 10 oz. cans)
- Black pepper (1 tbsp.)
- Salt (2 tsp.)
- Water (2 cups or as needed)
- Cayenne (as desired)

Method of Prep:

1. Gather the fixings. Drain the beans in a colander. Seed and dice the peppers. Mince the onion and garlic.
2. Add the ground beef to a large pot using med-high heat. Cook it until browned. Drain the grease and mix in the onions, bell peppers, and garlic. Simmer for about three minutes.
3. Toss the remainder of the fixings into the pan. Simmer using the low-heat temperature setting (lid off) until the meat is tender or

about one hour. Add more water as needed. Adjust the spices and serve hot.

Tips for Meal Prep:

1. Scoop the chili (1 cup) into a container or a plastic freezer bag. Seal, leaving ½ inch of empty space at the top.
2. Label it with the date you made it and also the time you placed it in the freezer. Usually, chilies that are frozen are good for one week.
3. Place each bag of chili at the end of the freezer, as this is the coldest part of the freezer.
4. To Eat: Thaw the chili in the refrigerator for 1 hour. Place it in a pot over medium heat (rolling boil). Keep the pot covered to retain moisture.
5. Upon boiling, lower the temperature. At this point, it's necessary to season it because the flavor has diminished a little during the freezing process.
6. Serve it piping hot.

Dinner: Cajun Chicken

Yields Provided: 4-5

Ingredients for Prep:

- Chicken breast (1 lb.)
- Black pepper (1 pinch)
- Olive oil (1 tbsp.)
- Dried oregano (.5 tsp.)
- Low-sodium vegetable stock (.25 cup)
- Cajun seasoning (1 tbsp.)
- Chopped green onions (4)
- Cherry tomatoes - cut in half (2 cups)
- Minced cloves of garlic (3)
- Coconut cream (.66 cup)
- Sweet paprika (.5 tsp.)
- Lemon juice (2 tbsp.)

Method of Prep:
1. Heat a skillet using the med-high temperature setting.
2. Once the oil is hot, toss in the chicken and portion of pepper. Cook on each side for five (5) minutes.
3. Pour in the stock, oregano, lemon juice, cream, paprika, garlic, green onions, and the Cajun seasoning.
4. Simmer for about ten minutes. Divide into serving bowls and enjoy.

Tips for Meal Prep:
1. Let everything cool.
2. Portion the fixings into storage containers to freeze.

Snack: Fruit Snack Pack

Yields Provided: 3 packs

Ingredients for Prep:
- Raspberries (.5 cup)
- Sliced oranges (¼ of 1)
- Strawberries (4)
- Grapes (1 cup)
- Trail mix (2 tbsp.)
- Foster Farms Bold Bites Pouch (1)

Method of Prep:
1. Slice the orange before you begin.

Tips for Meal Prep:
1. Add the trail mix to a reusable dipping container.

2. Fill a small reusable dipping sauce container with 2 tablespoons of the trail mix. Close the top tightly and transfer to a single-compartment container.
3. Arrange the prepared fruit (orange, strawberries, grapes, raspberries) within the container and cover.
4. Serve with 1 pouch of your favorite Bold Bites and store in the fridge until ready to enjoy.

Day 11

Breakfast: Carrot Muffins

Yields Provided: 5

Ingredients for Prep:

- Whole wheat flour (1.5 cups)
- Stevia/your preferred sweetener (.5 cup)
- Baking soda (.5 tsp.)
- Cinnamon (.5 tsp.)
- Baking powder (1 tsp.)
- Natural apple juice (.25 cup)
- Egg (1)
- Olive oil (.25 cup)
- Freshly picked cranberries (1 cup)
- Grated carrots (2)
- Chopped pecans (.25 cup)
- Grated ginger (2 tsp.)
- Cooking oil spray (as needed)

Method of Prep:

1. Warm the oven to reach 375° Fahrenheit.
2. Drain the cranberries.
3. Sift or whisk the stevia, flour, cinnamon, baking soda, and baking powder in a mixing container.
4. Pour in the apple juice, whisked egg, oil, cranberries, carrots, pecans, and ginger. Stir thoroughly.
5. Lightly grease a muffin tray with a spritz of cooking oil spray. Divide the mix and to each of the containers.
6. Bake for 30 minutes. When ready, take out of the oven.

Tips for Meal Prep:

1. Leave in the muffin pan for 5 to 10 minutes to cool.
2. Remove each muffin from the pan and thoroughly cool before storing it in the refrigerator. Freeze for longer storage.
3. If frozen, leave them on the countertop to defrost for about 30 minutes.
4. You can also add them in a lunchbox for a quick pick-up at work.

Lunch: Classic Stuffed Peppers

Yields Provided: 6

Ingredients for Prep:

- Green peppers (6 large)
- Lean ground beef (1 lb.)
- Onion (.25 cup)
- Diced tomatoes (16 oz. can)
- Tomato sauce (16 oz. can)
- Basil (1 tsp.)
- Oregano (1 tsp.)
- Black pepper & salt (as desired)
- Instant white rice (1 bag)
- Shredded cheddar cheese (1 cup)

Method of Prep:

1. Warm the oven in advance to reach 350° Fahrenheit.
2. Brown the beef and finely chopped onion in a large skillet using the low-temperature setting.
3. Slice the tops off of each pepper, discard the seeds, and arrange in a lightly greased baking dish.
4. Prepare the rice according to package instructions and drain.
5. In a large mixing container, combine the tomato sauce, basil, oregano, salt, black pepper, rice, and diced tomatoes. Stir in the cooked beef and onions with a few chopped peppers if desired.

6. Spoon the mixture into each shell. Bake for 35 minutes.
7. Remove and add a portion of cheddar cheese on top. Place back into the oven. Bake until the cheese has melted (5 min.).

Tips for Meal Prep:
1. Cool thoroughly and wrap each pepper in plastic wrap. Place into freezer zipper bags or individual containers to keep for up to six months.
2. Defrost them in the microwave when desired. Reheat them for five minutes. Remove the dish from the microwave and sprinkle with a portion of fresh cheese. Serve when ready.

Dinner: Cilantro Lime Chicken

Yields Provided: 6

Ingredients for Prep:
- Chicken breast (1 lb.)
- Orange juice (1 cup)
- Chicken broth (1 cup)
- Juice (2 fresh limes)
- Garlic (2 tsp.)
- Cilantro leaves (.5 cup)
- Black beans (1 can)
- Frozen corn (2 cups)
- Ground cumin (1 tbsp.)

Method of Prep:
1. Rinse and drain the beans, mince the garlic, and chop the cilantro leaves. Remove the skin and bones from the chicken.
2. This is great to prepare and set aside for those days when you are pressed for time. Add all ingredients to a gallon-sized freezer bag or container.

Tips for Meal Prep:

1. From thawed or freshly made, transfer into a slow cooker. Cook on high for three to four hours or low for six hours.
2. Serve as a homemade burrito bowl. Just add rice, sour cream, guacamole, and cilantro for a super delicious meal. Tacos and nachos are great ways to serve this as well.

Snack: Avocado Hummus Snack Jars

Yields Provided: 4 jars

Ingredients for Prep:

- Chickpeas (1 can)
- Tahini (.5 cup)
- Avocado (1)
- Garlic (2 cloves)
- Lemon juice (1 tbsp.)
- Salt (.5 tsp.)
- Water (.25 cup)
- Optional Toppings: Sliced sun-dried tomatoes/antipasto
- Celery, cucumber & carrot sticks
- Assorted chips & crackers

Method of Prep:

1. Rinse and drain the chickpeas. Dice the avocado and garlic. Cut the carrots, celery, and cucumber into wedges/sticks.
2. Toss all of the fixings (omit the optional/final toppings) into a Vitamix.
3. Blend using the lowest speed setting for about 30 seconds. Stir as needed until full mixed (5 min.).

Tips for Meal Prep:

1. Scoop into jam jars, and top with antipasto or sundried tomatoes.
2. Serve alongside cut-up veggies, crackers, chips, or whatever other snacks you're craving.
3. Enjoy within the first two to three days after preparation.

Day 12

Breakfast: Buckwheat Pancakes

Yields Provided: 6

Ingredients for Prep:

- All-purpose flour (.5 cup)
- Buckwheat flour (.5 cup)
- Baking powder (1 tbsp.)
- Sugar (1 tbsp.)
- Egg whites (2)
- Fat-free milk (.5 cup)
- Sparkling water (.5 cup)
- Fresh strawberries (3 cups)
- Canola oil (1 tbsp.)

Method of Prep:

1. Slice the berries. Whisk the oil, eggs, and milk in a small mixing container.
2. Use another dish to blend the sugar, baking powder, and each of the flours. Blend in the egg white mixture along with the water until barely moist.
3. Using the medium heat setting to prepare a nonstick griddle or skillet, and spoon the batter in ½ cup increments.
4. Continue cooking for about two minutes (bubbles will appear on the top).
5. Flip and continue to cook for about one to two more minutes.

Tips for Meal Prep:

1. Either serve now or cool for storage.
2. Store in freezer bags until ready to serve.
3. Place the frozen pancakes in a heated 375° Fahrenheit oven for 8-10 minutes.
4. Garnish each one with 1/2 of a cup of sliced berries and serve.

Lunch: One-Tray Caprese Pasta

Yields Provided: 2

Ingredients for Prep:

- Pasta (2 cups - cooked al dente)
- Onion (.75 cup)
- Marinara sauce (1 cup)
- Fresh basil (.33 cup)
- Black pepper and salt (1 tsp. each)
- Optional: Mozzarella cheese
- Also Needed: Aluminum foil (2 sheets @ 12 by 12)

Method of Prep:

1. Set oven to 400° Fahrenheit.
2. Chop the veggies and shred the cheese.
3. Stack the sheets of foil on top of each other.
4. Fold one side of the foil about ⅓ of the way across the sheet, repeat for the opposite side.
5. Pinch the corner to form a point and then flatten it to the short side of the foil, forming a raised corner. Repeat for all four sides (make 4).
6. Add all of the ingredients to the foil boats and stir.
7. Bake for 12 minutes.

Tips for Meal Prep:

1. Cool for 10-15 minutes.
2. Refrigerate for no longer than three to five days.

Dinner: Shrimp Taco Bowls

Yields Provided: 4

Ingredients for Prep:

Spicy Shrimp:
- Medium shrimp (20)
- Garlic clove (1 minced)
- Olive oil (1 tbsp.)
- Ground cumin (.5 tsp.)
- Chili powder (.5 tsp.)
- Optional: Onion powder (.25 tsp.)
- Kosher salt (.25 tsp.)

To Serve:
- Brown rice (2 cups - cooked)
- Corn (1 cup)
- Black beans (1 cup)
- Tomatoes (1 cup - diced)
- Cheddar cheese (.5 cup)
- Cilantro (2 tbsp. - minced)
- Lime (1 cut into 4 slices)
- Meal prep containers (4)

Method of Prep:
1. Drain and rinse the corn and black beans.
2. Peel and devein the shrimp. Toss them into a medium mixing bowl.
3. Whisk the olive oil, salt, cumin, garlic, chili powder, and onion powder. Fold in the shrimp and toss gently.
4. Cover and pop into the fridge to marinate for at least ten minutes or up to 24 hours.
5. Heat a large heavy-duty or cast-iron skillet using the high heat temperature setting for two minutes. Add the olive oil and shrimp.

6. Cook the shrimp in a skillet over med-high heat until pink and cooked thoroughly (5 min.)

Tips for Meal Prep:
1. Divide the brown rice into four containers (.5 cup each). Top with five shrimp, corn, tomatoes, a scoop of black beans, cheese, cilantro, and a lime wedge.
2. Cover and place in the fridge for a maximum of four days.
3. Time to Eat: Warm the bowls in the microwave for two minutes or until heated thoroughly. Top with salsa, sour cream, or guacamole to your liking along with a drizzle of lime juice.

Snack: Vanilla Cashew Butter Cups

Yields Provided: 12 large or 24 small cups

Ingredients for Prep:
- Dark chocolate or chocolate chips (7 oz. - chopped)
- Cashew butter (1 cup)
- Honey/maple syrup for vegan (2 tbsp.)
- Vanilla (1 tbsp.)
- Sea salt (1 pinch)
- Flaky sea salt - for the tops
- Also Needed: 12-count or 24-count muffin tin with liners

Method of Prep:
1. Line the muffin tin with liners.
2. Place about two-thirds of the chocolate in a pan using the low-temperature heat setting. After it's mostly melted, remove it from the heat and add the remaining chocolate. Stir a few times while the residual heat melts the chocolate.
3. Working one at a time, add slightly less than a tablespoon of the melted chocolate to one of the cupcake liners. Tip it on its side and rotate it so that the chocolate comes one-third of the way up

the side of the liner. Repeat until all the liners have a chocolate coating then place them in the fridge to harden.

4. Add the cashew butter, honey, vanilla, and salt to a medium-sized bowl. Gently fold them together. Once the chocolate cups have hardened, divide the cashew butter between the cups. Use your finger to press it down into the cups.

5. Pour the remaining chocolate over the tops of the cashew butter cups, then pop them back into the fridge to harden.

6. Sprinkle a little flaky sea salt on top to make them irresistible.

Tips for Meal Prep:

1. In a microwave, melt the chocolate for 20 to 30 seconds. Drizzle and serve.

2. Cashew butter can be pricey. You can make your own with a food processor or high-powered blender and about ten minutes. You'll need two cups of raw cashews plus one tablespoon of coconut oil to make 1 cup of cashew butter.

Day 13

Breakfast: Corn & Apple Muffins

Yields Provided: 12

Ingredients for Prep:

- All-purpose flour (2 cups)
- Packed brown sugar (.25 cup)
- Yellow cornmeal (.5 cup)
- Baking powder (1 tbsp.)
- Salt (.25 tsp.)
- Egg whites (2)
- Apple (1)
- Corn kernels (.5 cup)

Method of Prep:

1. Peel and coarsely chop the apple.
2. Use a 12-cup muffin pan and line the containers with foil or paper liners.
3. Set the oven temperature to reach 425° Fahrenheit.
4. Mix the brown sugar, cornmeal, salt, flour, and baking powder completely in a big container.
5. Use a separate mixing container to beat the egg whites and milk. Blend in the corn kernels and apple bits.
6. Whisk again and pour the batter into the flour mixture. Continue to gently stir the fixings until slightly moistened.
7. Fill the cups 2/3 of the way full. Bake for about 30 minutes.
8. Test the muffins for doneness by gently pressing the center. They should spring back.

Tips for Meal Prep:

1. Cool thoroughly before placing the muffins into a storage container.
2. Store in the fridge for longer storage times.

Lunch: Smoked Sausage & Orzo

Yields Provided: 6-8

Ingredients for Prep:

- Jennie-O Hardwood Smoked Turkey Sausage (16 oz.)
- Olive oil (1 tbsp.)
- Yellow onion (1 small)
- Red bell pepper (1 small)
- Garlic (3 cloves)
- Cajun seasoning (1 tbsp.)
- Crushed red pepper flakes (.5 tbsp.)
- Chicken broth - Low-sodium (14.5 oz. can)
- Crushed tomatoes (15 oz. can)
- Uncooked orzo pasta (8 oz.)
- Medium zucchini (1 shredded)
- Kosher salt (.5 tsp.)
- Freshly cracked black pepper (as desired)
- For the Garnish: Flat-leaf parsley

Method of Prep:

1. Slice the sausage diagonally and add to a large skillet with olive oil. Dice and toss in the onions, bell peppers, garlic, kosher salt, black pepper, Cajun seasoning, and pepper flakes.
2. Pour in the chicken broth, orzo, and tomatoes. Wait for it to boil.
3. Reduce the heat setting to med-low and cover. Set a timer for 8 minutes, or until the orzo is tender.

Tips for Meal Prep:

1. Pour the fixings into resealable plastic bags or shallow airtight containers for up to three to five days.
2. Time to Eat: Stir in shredded zucchini, freshly chop flat-leaf Italian parsley and a sprinkle of Cajun seasoning.

Dinner: Chicken & Broccoli

Yields Provided: 4

Ingredients for Prep:

- Breasts of chicken (4)
- Olive oil (1 tbsp.)
- Red onions (1 cup)
- Garlic cloves (2)
- Oregano (1 tbsp.)
- Coconut cream (.5 cup)
- Broccoli florets (2 cups)

Method of Prep:

1. Cut the skin and bones from the chicken breasts.
2. Mince the garlic cloves. Chop the red onions and oregano.
3. Heat a skillet to warm the oil using the med-high heat setting.
4. Arrange the chicken breasts in the pan and simmer for about 5 minutes per side.
5. Toss in the onions and garlic. Stir and cook for approximately 5 more minutes.
6. Add in the broccoli, cream, and oregano. Continue cooking for 10 more minutes.
7. When ready, portion into the plates and serve.

Tips for Meal Prep:

1. It will keep for 3-5 days in the fridge.
2. For further prep time, cover with foil and place in a freezer bag or container.

Snack: Protein Snack Pack

Yields Provided: 3

Ingredients for Prep:

- Foster Farms <u>Bold Bites</u> Pouch
- Hard-Boiled egg (1)
- Chopped cheese (.25 cup)
- Avocado (half of 1)
- Chickpeas (.5 cup)
- Hazelnuts/your preference (2 tbsp.)

Method of Prep:
1. Chop the cheese into cubes.
2. Fill a dipping sauce <u>container</u> with two tablespoons of hazelnuts.
3. Close the top and place it into a storage container alongside the rest of the fixings.

Tips for Meal Prep:
1. Arrange the egg, chickpeas, cheese, and avocado within the storage container and securely close the lid or use plastic wrap.
2. Place in the fridge until needed. It's best used within 24 to 48 hours.
3. When it is time to eat, serve with a pouch of the bold bites.

Day 14

Breakfast: Veggies & Eggs

Yields Provided: 4

Ingredients for Prep:

- Large eggs (8)
- Broccoli crowns (2)
- Small head cauliflower (half of 1)
- Bell peppers (2)
- Garlic powder (1 tsp.)
- Black pepper (as desired)
- Salt (.5 tsp.)
- Avocado/coconut oil (3 tbsp.)
- Water (.25 cup)
- Optional: Cheese of choice
- Sprouted bread slices (2 toasted)
- For Serving: Salsa

Method of Prep:

1. Coarsely chop the broccoli and cauliflower. Dice the peppers.
2. Warm a large ceramic skillet using the medium temperature heat setting and swirl two tablespoons of oil to coat. Toss in the broccoli and cauliflower. Cover and cook for two to three minutes. Stir, cover, and cook for another two to three minutes.
3. Meanwhile, in a small dish, whisk the eggs, water, pepper, and ¼ teaspoon of salt. Whisk well and set aside.
4. Add the bell pepper, rest of the salt, garlic powder, and black pepper to the skillet with the vegetables. Stir and cook for two to three more minutes.

Tips for Meal Prep:
1. Divide between four plastic or glass meal prep containers, add a small container of salsa, 1/2 slice of toast, and sprinkle of cheese if desired.
2. Refrigerate for up to 5 days. Heat in a skillet on the stovetop.
3. Swirl one tablespoon of oil into the pan and pour in the egg mixture. Cook until it's scrambled, stirring (folding) constantly.

Lunch: Starbucks™ Protein Bistro Box

Yields Provided: 8

Ingredients for Prep:

- Hard-boiled eggs (8)
- Grapes (2 cups)
- Large apples (2)
- Mini Babybel cheese - Reduced-fat (4)
- Multi-grain flatbread sandwich thins (2 cuts in quarters)
- Honey-Roasted Peanut Butter (portioned into 2 oz. containers)
- Optional: Freshly squeezed lemon juice
- Freshly cracked pepper and kosher salt (as desired)

Method of Prep:
1. Rinse the apples and grapes. Brush the apple slices lightly using the juice to prevent browning.
2. Boil and peel the eggs. Cool and dust eggs using salt and pepper to taste.

Tips for Meal Prep:
1. Assemble the protein bistro boxes and store refrigerated.
2. It is recommended to store the eggs whole.

Dinner: Sweet & Sour Meatballs

Yields Provided: 8-12

Ingredients for Prep:

- *The Meatballs*:
- Ground chuck (1.5 lb.)
- Water chestnuts (3-4 tbsp. - chopped)
- Quick oats (.75 cup)
- Garlic powder (.5 tsp.)
- Onion powder (.5 tsp.)
- Salt (.5 tsp.)
- Egg (1 beaten)
- Milk (.5 cup)
- Soy sauce - reduced-sodium (.5 tsp.)
- *The Sauce:*
- Brown sugar (1 cup)
- Beef bouillon (.5 cup)
- Vinegar (.5 cup)
- Cornstarch (2 tbsp.)
- Reduced-sodium soy sauce (2 tsp.)
- Pineapple tidbits - drained (8-9 oz. can)
- Chopped bell pepper - green (.5 cup)

Method of Prep:

1. Combine the meatball fixings preparing them into one-inch balls.
2. Brown, drain the grease and set aside.
3. Whisk the sugar, vinegar, bouillon, cornstarch, and soy sauce in a Dutch oven or large deep skillet, bringing it to a boil.
4. Simmer the sauce mixture until thickened. Drain and stir in the pineapple, peppers, and meatballs.
5. Continue cooking for about half an hour.

Tips for Meal Prep:

1. Cool the meatballs until thoroughly chilled.
2. Measure your required number of meatballs per serving into a freezer bag.
3. Pop the package into the freezer for a quick meal.
4. Be sure to label it with its contents and date to ensure you don't overlook it.

Snack: Ham – Swiss & Spinach Roll-Ups

Yields Provided: 1

Ingredients for Prep:

- Uncured organic deli ham/your preference (1 slice)
- Hummus (1 tbsp.)
- Swiss cheese (half of 1 slice)
- Baby spinach leaves (4-5)

Method of Prep:
1. Spread hummus onto the slice of ham.
2. Top that with swiss cheese and spinach leaves.
3. Roll them up.

Tips for Meal Prep:
1. Prepare as many snacks as you want to prep.
2. The roll-ups can be made 1-2 days ahead of time.

Chapter 4:
Keto Diet

What Is the Keto Diet?

The term keto in ketogenic comes from ketones. Ketones are small fuel molecules produced in the body. These molecules provide an alternative source of fuel for the body when there's a short supply of glucose in the blood.

When you consume very few carbs, your body will not have sufficient glucose or blood sugar needed to power the cells. Since glucose is unavailable, the body will reach into its fat reserves to produce blood sugar.

The ketogenic process takes place in the liver. It is the liver that produces ketones from fat stores in the body. These ketones then provide the necessary fuel needed throughout the body and mostly for the brain. The brain is an organ that is continuously working and has a high demand for energy. However, it cannot run on fat. It only functions on glucose or ketones.

When you consume no carbs, the body will lack glucose to produce energy, and the body will convert the fat that you consume into ketones. This happens when your insulin levels fall drastically. When this happens, fat burning occurs quite fast. Your body can easily access stored fat, including the stubborn fat around the belly and waistline.

The ketogenic process is excellent for weight loss and fat burning. If you are looking to lose weight and shed off the pounds, then the ketogenic diet is highly recommended. However, apart from the benefit of weight loss occasioned by the keto diet, you will also enjoy a host of other benefits as well. For instance, you will lose weight but without the need to fast.

Variations of the Ketogenic Diet Plan

- **Standard Ketogenic Diet**: It's also known as SKD, which is a high-fat, very low-carb, and moderate-protein diet. This diet consists of 20% protein, 75% carbs, and only 5% carbs.

- **Targeted Ketogenic Diet:** The technique used in this dieting phase is similar to the standard keto diet except that it allows variations in carbs intake based on workout demands.

- **Cyclic Ketogenic Diet:** This variation of the keto diet involves varying periods where you enjoy five days of ketogenic diet followed by two days where you have a diet high in carbs; hence, the 5:2 diet.

- ***High-Protein Ketogenic Diet:*** You can also enjoy a high-protein keto diet, which is somewhat similar to the standard keto diet. However, it consists of higher protein levels compared to the SKD diet. The ratios here are 35% protein, 60% fat, and 5% carbs.

Most people follow the standard ketogenic diet and sometimes the high-protein keto diet. For purposes of learning more about the ketogenic diet, we will focus more on the standard version.

Benefits of the Keto Diet

Ketosis has numerous benefits. At the onset, it provides the brain and body an endless supply of energy. This energy is crucial for the brain and helps you to be sharp and focused. This also enhances your physical and mental endurance.

Other benefits of ketosis include the facilitation of effortless weight loss. Ketosis is one of the most efficient weight loss processes known. People who have type 2 diabetes can get relief from the condition. Type II diabetes is aggravated by excessive blood sugar, which is controlled via ketosis. Other conditions, such as epilepsy, can easily be controlled using ketosis even without the use of medication.

Let's see how tasty the foods are in this segment! You'll be surprised!

Week 1

Day 1

Breakfast: Almost McGriddle Casserole

Yields Provided: 8

Total Net Carbs: 3 grams

Ingredients for Prep:

- Breakfast sausage (1 lb.)
- Flaxseed meal (.25 cup)
- Almond flour (1 cup)
- Large eggs (10)
- Maple syrup (6 tbsp.)
- Cheese (4 oz.)
- Butter (4 tbsp.)
- Onion (.5 tsp.)
- Sage (.25 tsp.)
- Garlic powder (.5 tsp.)
- *Also Needed*: 9 by 9-inch casserole dish & parchment baking paper

Method of Prep:

1. Warm the oven temperature to reach 350° Fahrenheit.
2. Use the medium heat setting on the stovetop to prepare the sausage in a skillet.
3. Add all of the dry fixings (the cheese also), and stir in the wet ones. Add four tablespoons of syrup. Stir and blend well.
4. After the sausage is browned, combine everything (the grease too).

5. Prepare the casserole dish using a sheet of baking paper. Dump the mixture into the casserole dish. Drizzle using the rest of the syrup and bake for 45 to 55 minutes.
6. Transfer to the countertop to cool.

Tips for Meal Prep:
1. The casserole should be easily removed by using the edge of the parchment paper.
2. After the casserole has cooled, slice it into eight portions to enjoy for a couple of days.
3. Place the muffins in a storage container or freezer baggie. Store in the fridge for about five days or freeze for later.

Lunch: Caesar Salmon Salad

Yields Provided: 2

Total Carbohydrates: 2 grams

Ingredients for Prep:

- Salmon fillets (2 - 6 oz. portions)
- Bacon slices (4)
- Ghee (1 tbsp. or as needed)
- Pink salt (1 pinch)
- Freshly ground black pepper (1 pinch)
- Avocado (.5 of 1)
- Romaine hearts (2 cups)
- Caesar dressing (2 tbsp.)

Method of Prep:
1. Cook the bacon until crispy for 8 minutes using the med-high heat setting on the stovetop. Drain on a platter using paper towels.
2. Remove the excess water from the fillets. Give them a shake of pepper and salt.

3. Use the same pan to prepare the salmon. Add butter if needed.
4. Cook the salmon for five minutes per side for medium-rare.

Tips for Meal Prep:
1. Break the bacon into bits.
2. Chop the romaine hearts and slice the avocado.
3. Prepare two salad dishes or a closed container for the meal prep with equal parts of romaine, avocado, and the bacon.
4. Place the bacon into separate containers to keep them crunchy.
5. When ready to serve, enjoy with a drizzle of the dressing.

Dinner: Chipotle Roast

Yields Provided: 4

Total Carbohydrates: 1 gram

Ingredients for Prep:

- Diced tomatoes (7.25 oz.)
- Bone broth (6 oz.)
- Diced green chilis (2 oz.)
- Pork roast (2 lb.)
- Chipotle powder (1 tsp.)
- Cumin (.5 tsp.)
- Onion powder (.5 tsp.)

Method of Prep:
1. Combine each of the fixings in the Instant Pot and close the lid
2. Manually set the timer for 1 hour. Natural-release the pressure

Tips for Meal Prep:
1. Cool the roast and slice into four portions.
2. Freeze in individual compartment storage containers. Add your favorite vegetable and freeze for later.

3. When it's dinner time, defrost the meat, and heat as desired.

Snack: Peanut Butter Protein Bars

Yields Provided: 12 bars

Total Carbohydrates: 3 grams

Ingredients for Prep:

- Keto-friendly chunky peanut butter (1 cup)
- Egg whites (2)
- Almonds (.5 cup)
- Cashews (.5 cup)
- Almond meal (1.5 cups)

Method of Prep:
1. Warm up the oven ahead of time to 350° Fahrenheit.
2. Combine all of the fixings and add them to the prepared dish.
3. Bake for 15 minutes, and cut into 12 pieces once they're cooled.

Tips for Meal Prep:
1. Store in the fridge to keep them fresh using a closed, airtight container.

Day 2

Breakfast: Jalapeno Cheddar Waffles

Yields Provided: 1

Total Carbohydrates: 6 grams

Ingredients for Prep:

- Large eggs (3)
- Jalapeno (1 small)
- Cream cheese (3 oz.)
- Psyllium husk powder (1 tsp.)
- Coconut flour (1 tbsp.)
- Cheddar cheese (1 oz.)
- Baking powder (1 tsp.)
- *Also Needed:* Immersion blender

Method of Prep:

1. Mix all of the fixings using the blender, except for the jalapeno and cheese.
2. After you have a smooth texture, add the cheese and jalapeno Blend and pour the batter into the waffle iron.
3. Cook for 5 to 6 minutes. Set aside when done.

Tips for Meal Prep:

1. Let the waffles cool off for prep.
2. Put them into a plastic freezer bag and pop them in the freezer until you have the desire for a delicious waffle.
3. To reheat, preheat the oven temperature to 400° Fahrenheit When it's hot, place the waffles on a baking tin. Warm them up for 5 minutes. Serve and enjoy!
4. *Tip*: It isn't recommended to warm them in a regular toaster.

Lunch: Chicken 'Zoodle' Soup

Yields Provided: 2

Total Carbohydrates: 4 grams

Ingredients for Prep:
- Chicken broth (3 cups)
- Chicken breast (1)
- Avocado oil (2 tbsp.)
- Green onion (1)
- Celery stalk (1)
- Cilantro (.25 cup)
- Salt (to taste)
- Peeled zucchini (1)

Method of Prep:
1. Chop or dice the breast of the chicken. Pour the oil into a saucepan and cook the chicken until done. Pour in the broth and simmer.
2. Chop the celery and green onions and toss into the pan. Simmer for 3 to 4 more minutes.
3. Chop the cilantro and prepare the zucchini noodles. Use a spiralizer or potato peeler to make the 'noodles.' Add to the pot.
4. Simmer for a few more minutes and season to your liking.

Tips for Meal Prep:
1. Store in a glass container in the fridge. It will remain tasty for 2 to 3 days.

Dinner: Chicken Nuggets

Yields Provided: 6

Total Carbohydrates: 2 grams

Ingredients for Prep:

- Cooked chicken (2 cups)
- Cream cheese (8 oz.)
- Egg (1)
- Garlic salt (1 tsp.)
- Almond flour (.25 cup)

Method of Prep:

1. Set the oven temperature to 350° Fahrenheit.
2. Lightly spritz a baking tray using a misting of cooking oil spray. You can also use a layer of parchment paper.
3. Shred the chicken using a food processor or by hand. (Try using a combination of dark and light meat.)
4. Combine the rest of the fixings and mix well.
5. Scoop the nugget mixture onto the baking tin.
6. Bake until firm and slightly browned (12 to 14 min.).

Tips for Meal Prep:

1. You will love this one. Just prepare the mixture and bake.
2. Store in the fridge for one or two days.
3. Freeze and enjoy at another time for lunch, dinner, or just a snack

Snack: Blueberry Cream Cheese Fat Bombs

Yields Provided: 12

Total Carbohydrates: 1 gram

Ingredients for Prep:

- Unchilled cream cheese (1.5 cups)
- Fresh/frozen berries (1 cup)
- Swerve (2-3 tbsp.)
- Vanilla extract (1 tbsp.)
- Coconut oil (.5 cup)

Method of Prep:

1. About 30 to 60 minutes before preparation time, place the cream cheese on the countertop to become room temperature.
2. Take the stems off the berries and rinse. Pour into a blender. Mix well until smooth.
3. Pour in the Swerve and extract. Blend in the oil and cream cheese.
4. Add the mixture to candy molds and freeze for approximately two hours.

Tips for Meal Prep:

1. Once the bombs are solid, just pop them out.
2. Store in freezer bags or another safe freezer container.

Day 3

Breakfast: Baked Green Eggs

Yields Provided: 6

Total Carbohydrates: 5 grams

Ingredients for Prep:

- Sun-dried tomatoes (.25 cup)
- Feta cheese (.5 cup)
- Oregano (.5 tsp.)
- Chopped kale (1 cup)
- Eggs (12)

Method of Prep:

1. Warm up the oven to reach 350° Fahrenheit.
2. Cover a baking tin with a layer of foil and a spritz of nonstick cooking spray.
3. Whisk the eggs and combine with the rest of the fixings. Stir well and pour into the pan to bake for approximately 25 minutes.
4. Transfer to the countertop to entirely cool and slice.

Tips for Meal Prep:

1. Place the package in the refrigerator to use within four to five days in an airtight container.
2. You can also place them into individual containers for convenience.

Lunch: Mushroom & Cauliflower Risotto

Yields Provided: 4

Total Carbohydrates: 4 grams

Ingredients for Prep:

- Cauliflower (1)
- Vegetable stock (1 cup)
- Chopped mushrooms (9 oz.)
- Butter (2 tbsp.)
- Coconut cream (1 cup)
- Pepper and Salt (to taste)

Method of Prep:

1. Pour the stock in a saucepan. Boil and set aside.
2. Prepare a skillet with butter and sauté the mushrooms until golden.
3. Grate and stir in the cauliflower and stock.

Tips for Meal Prep:

1. Simmer and add the cream, cooking until the cauliflower is al dente. Serve.
2. Let it cool before placing it in the fridge for storage.

Dinner: Chili Lime Cod

Yields Provided: 2

Total Carbohydrates: 3 grams

Ingredients for Prep:

- Wild-caught cod (10-12 oz.)
- Coconut flour (.33 cup)
- Egg (3)
- Lime (1)
- Garlic powder (1 tsp.)
- Cayenne pepper (.5 tsp.
- Salt (1 tsp.)
- Crushed red pepper (1 tsp.)

Method of Prep:
1. Heat the oven temperature to reach 400° Fahrenheit.
2. In separate dishes, whip the egg, and remove any lumps from the flour.
3. Let the fillet soak in the egg dish for one minute per side. Dip it into the flour dish, and then add it to a baking sheet.
4. Sprinkle the spices and drizzle the lime juice over the cod, and bake it for 10 to 12 minutes or when it easily flakes apart.

Tips for Meal Prep:
1. Cool the fish entirely once it is like you like it.
2. Use foil to keep the fish safe for a day. Freeze and enjoy later.
3. Once it is time to eat, just drizzle with some Sriracha if you wish, and enjoy.

Snack: Coffee Fat Bombs

Yields Provided: 15

Total Carbohydrates: 0 grams

Ingredients for Prep:

- Unchilled cream cheese (4.4 oz.)
- Powdered xylitol (2 tbsp.)
- Instant coffee (1 tbsp.)
- Unsweetened cocoa powder (1 tbsp.)
- Coconut oil (1 tbsp.)
- Unchilled butter (1 tbsp.)

Method of Prep:

1. Put the butter and cream cheese on the countertop for about an hour before it's time to begin.
2. Use a blender/food processor to blitz the xylitol and coffee into a fine powder. Add the hot water to form a pasty mix.
3. Blend in the cream cheese, cocoa powder, butter, and coconut oil.
4. Add to ice cube trays and freeze for a minimum of one to two hours.

Tips for Meal Prep:

1. Use zipper-type bags to keep them fresh in the freezer.

Day 4

Breakfast: Vegan Gingerbread Muffins

Yields Provided: 5

Total Carbohydrates: 2 grams

Ingredients for Prep:

- Non-dairy milk or water (.75 cup)
- Granulated sweetener - your preference (.25 cup)
- Ground flax seeds (.5 cup)
- Melted coconut oil or MCT oil (2 tbsp.)
- Vanilla extract (1 tsp.)
- Coconut flour (.5 cup)
- Freshly grated ginger (1.5 tsp.)
- Allspice (.25 tsp.)
- Cinnamon (1.5 tsp.)
- Ground cloves (.25 tsp.)
- Nutmeg (.25 tsp.)
- *Also Needed*: Standard-size muffin pan with paper liners

Method of Prep:

1. Heat the oven to 375° Fahrenheit.
2. Line five of the wells of the pan with a layer of parchment baking paper.
3. Combine the sweetener, flax seeds, oil, milk, and vanilla. Whisk well and set aside for approximately five minutes for the seeds to rest.
4. In another mixing container, whisk the remainder of the fixings until the mixture has thickened.
5. Empty the batter mixture into the muffin pan.
6. Bake until the tops are firm to the touch (30-35 min.).

Tips for Meal Prep:

1. Remove and transfer to the countertop to cool in the pan for at least 15 minutes.
2. Once cool, the muffins should easily pop out of the pan.
3. Place the container in the refrigerator for the best storage results.

Lunch: Spicy Beef Wraps

Yields Provided: 2

Total Carbohydrates: 4 grams

Ingredients for Prep:

- Coconut oil (1-2 tbsp.)
- Onion (¼ of 1)
- Ground beef (.66 lb.)
- Chopped cilantro (2 tbsp.)
- Red bell pepper (1)
- Fresh ginger (1 tsp.)
- Cumin (2 tsp.)
- Garlic cloves (4)
- Pepper and salt (as preferred)
- Large cabbage leaves (8)

Method of Prep:
1. Dice the bell pepper, onion, ginger, and garlic.
2. Heat a frying pan and pour in the oil.
3. Sauté the peppers, onions, and ground beef using medium heat.
4. When done, add the pepper, salt, cumin, ginger, cilantro, and garlic.

Tips for Meal Prep:
1. Cool the burger entirely and add to storage containers.
2. *Time to Eat:* Prepare a large pot of boiling water (3/4 full).

3. Cook each leaf for 20 seconds, plunge it in cold water and drain before placing it on your serving dish.
4. Reheat the beef mixture.
5. Scoop the mixture onto each leaf, fold, and enjoy.

Dinner: Asparagus & Chicken

Yields Provided: 8

Total Carbohydrates: 4 grams

Ingredients for Prep:
- Chicken breasts (4 lbs.)
- Avocado oil (1 tbsp.)
- Trimmed asparagus (1 lb.)
- Sun-dried tomatoes (4)
- Thick-cut bacon slices (4)
- Salt (1 tsp.)
- Pepper (.25 tsp.)
- Provolone cheese slices (8)
- *Also Needed*: 1 baking pan

Method of Prep:
1. Slice the chicken into eight thin pieces. Chop the bacon and tomatoes into one-inch pieces.
2. Warm up the oven temperature to 400° Fahrenheit.
3. Add the oil to the baking pan along with the chicken and asparagus. Top it off with the tomatoes and bacon. Sprinkle some pepper and salt for seasoning.
4. Bake until the chicken reaches 160° Fahrenheit internally - or about 25 minutes.
5. Toss in the asparagus and cheese.
6. Garnish with some bacon and tomatoes. Bake another three to four minutes until the cheese has melted.

Tips for Meal Prep:

1. Prepare the chicken and store it in the fridge for several days.
2. Place into plastic bins or freezer bags until ready to use.
3. Prepare the asparagus when ready to eat and combine with the cheese. Garnish and serve.

Snack: Mocha Cheesecake Bars

Yields Provided: 16

Total Carbohydrates: 3 grams

Ingredients for Prep:

- Vanilla extract (2 tsp.)
- Unsalted butter (6 tbsp.)
- Large eggs (3)
- Almond flour (1.5 cups)
- Hershey's Baking Cocoa (.5 cup)
- Erythritol (1 cup)
- Salt (.5 tsp.)
- Instant coffee (.5 tbsp.)
- Baking powder (1 tsp.)

The Cream Cheese Layer

- Erythritol (.5 cup)
- Softened cream cheese (1 lb.)
- Large egg (1)
- Vanilla extract (1 tsp.)
- Also Needed: 8 by 8-inch baking pan

Method of Prep:

1. Heat the oven to 350° Fahrenheit. Lightly grease or spray the pan with a spritz of oil cooking spray.
2. Combine the wet fixings, starting with the vanilla, butter, and eggs.

3. In another container, combine the dry fixings and whisk with the wet ones. Reserve .25 cup of the batter for later. Pour the mixture into the pan.
4. Mix the cream cheese (room temperature) with the rest of the ingredients for the second layer. Spread it on the layer of brownies.
5. Use the reserved batter as the last layer (will be thin). Bake it for 30 to 35 minutes.

Tips for Meal Prep:
1. When cooled, slice the cheesecake bars.
2. They will store in the refrigerator for several days or freeze in containers or freezer bags for extended use. Be sure to date and add the name of the contents.

Day 5

Breakfast: Egg Loaf

Yields Provided: 6

Total Carbohydrates: 0 grams

Ingredients for Prep:

- Eggs (6)
- Water for steaming (2 cups)
- Unsalted butter (for the bowl)

Method of Prep:

1. Prepare a heat-proof container with the butter.
2. Break the eggs into the dish (yolks intact) and cover with a sheet of aluminum foil. Set aside.
3. Add the trivet and two cups of water into the Instant Pot cooker. Arrange the bowl in the cooker.
4. Secure the lid and choose the manual pressure cooker function for 4 minutes using the high-temperature setting.
5. When the egg loaf is done, quick-release the pressure, and remove the pot.

Tips for Meal Prep:

1. Let it cool slightly and place in the refrigerator for up to four days.
2. Chop to your liking and mix with a little egg for salad or a little butter, pepper, and salt.

Lunch: *BARBECUE Pork Loin*

Yields Provided: 4

Total Carbohydrates: 3 grams

Ingredients for Prep:

- Pork loin (1 lb.)
- Tomato paste (4 tbsp.)
- Worcestershire sauce (1 tsp.)
- Avocado oil (2 tbsp.)
- Smoked paprika (.5 tsp.)
- Minced garlic (.5 tsp.
- Chopped onion (1 tbsp.)

Method of Prep:

1. Whisk the minced garlic, chopped onion, paprika, tomato paste, and Worcestershire sauce. Use the rub to prepare the pork and wrap it in foil.
2. Marinate the pork loin in the fridge for at least 1/2 hour for the spices to be absorbed.
3. Add the trivet to the Instant Pot and pour the water into the cooker. Secure the lid.
4. Set the timer for 60 minutes. Natural-release the pressure, when it's done.

Tips for Meal Prep:

1. Open the lid and let it cool slightly.
2. Let the pork completely cool.
3. Place into individual containers along with your favorite prepped veggie.
4. When it's time to eat, just thaw the container.
5. Warm it up and serve as desired.

Dinner: Short Ribs

Yields Provided: 4

Total Carbohydrates: 2.5 grams

Ingredients for Prep:

- Keto-friendly soy sauce (.25 cup)
- Beef short ribs (6 - 4 oz. each)
- Fish sauce (2 tbsp.)
- Rice vinegar (2 tbsp.)
- Red pepper flakes (.5 tsp.)
- Sesame seeds (.5 tsp.)
- Onion powder (.5 tsp.)
- Salt (1 tbsp.)
- Minced garlic (.5 tsp.)
- Ground ginger (1 tsp.)
- Cardamom (.25 tsp.)

Method of Prep:

1. Mix the fish sauce, vinegar, and alternative soy sauce.
2. Arrange the ribs in a dish with high sides. Add the sauce and marinate for up to 1 hour.
3. Combine all of the spices together. Take the ribs from the dish and sprinkle with the rub.
4. Warm up the grill (med-high) and cook for three to five minutes per side.

Tips for Meal Prep:

1. Put the ribs in a platter to cool.
2. Place in freezer bags or into plastic containers (4 portions) until it's time to serve and enjoy.

Snack: Delicious No-Bake Coconut Cookies

Yields Provided: 20

Total Carbohydrates: 0 grams

Ingredients for Prep:

- Melted coconut oil (1 cup)
- Monk fruit sweetened maple syrup or sweetener of choice (.5 cup)
- Shredded unsweetened coconut flakes (3 cups)

Method of Prep:

1. Prepare a cookie tray with a layer of parchment baking paper.
2. Combine all of the fixings. Run your hands through some water from the tap and shape the mixture into small balls. Arrange them in the pan around one to two inches apart.
3. Press them down to form a cookie and refrigerate until firm.

Tips for Meal Prep:

1. Prepare these into individual bags if you're an on-the-go kind of person.
2. The cookies will remain fresh covered for up to 7 days at room temperature.
3. Store in the fridge for up to a month.
4. If you choose, you can freeze the cookies for up to two months.

Day 6

Breakfast: Spinach Quiche

Yields Provided: 6

Total Carbohydrates: 0 grams

Ingredients for Prep:

- Chopped onion (1)
- Olive oil (1 tbsp.)
- Frozen & thawed spinach (10 oz. pkg.)
- Shredded muenster cheese (3 cups)
- Organic eggs – whisked (5)
- To Taste: Black pepper and salt
- Also Needed: 9-inch pie plate

Method of Prep:

1. Heat the oven at 350° Fahrenheit. Lightly grease the dish.
2. Use the medium temperature setting to warm a skillet with the oil.
3. Toss in the onion and sauté for 4-5 minutes. Raise the heat setting to med-high.
4. Fold in the spinach. Sauté for about two to three minutes or until the liquid is absorbed. Cool slightly.
5. Combine the rest of the fixings in a large mixing container, and toss with the cooled spinach. Dump into the prepared dish. Set a timer to bake for 30 minutes.
6. Take the quiche out of the oven to cool for at least ten minutes.
7. Slice into six wedges.

Tips for Meal Prep:

1. Add the cooled pieces into plastic baggies.
2. It will store in the fridge for two to four days.

3. To warm up, prepare in the microwave for one minute on the high setting before serving.

Lunch: BLT Salad in a Jar

Yields Provided: 8

Total Carbohydrates: 7 grams

Ingredients for Prep:

- Romaine lettuce (2 cups)
- Iceberg lettuce (2 cups)
- Chopped scallions (2)
- Diced tomatoes (2)
- Bacon slices (4 crumbled)

Method of Prep:
1. Combine all of the dressing components.
2. Slowly pour into the jars.
3. Layer the veggies, croutons, and garnish of bacon.

Tips for Meal Prep:
1. Tightly close each of the jars.
2. Place in the refrigerator and enjoy it within three days.

Dinner: Buffalo Chicken Burgers

Yields Provided: 2 burgers

Total Carbohydrates: 1 gram

Ingredients for Prep:

- Cooked chicken breasts (8 oz.)
- Room-temperature cream cheese (2 oz.)
- Shredded mozzarella cheese (.5 cup)
- Frank's Red-Hot Sauce or your choice (2 tbsp.)
- For Frying: Ghee or Coconut oil

Method of Prep:

1. Either chop or shred the prepared chicken and combine it with the rest of the fixings.
2. Place the fixings in the microwave for 15 to 20 seconds to help compact the ingredients. Form two medium patties and place them on a plate. Store in the freezer for about 15 minutes.
3. Heat a skillet using the high heat setting. Add the fat and patties. Prepare the burgers for 2 to 3 minutes per side.
4. Serve when crispy brown.

Tips for Meal Prep:

1. Prepare the chicken and shape the mixture into patties.
2. Freeze, or cook and freeze the patties.

Snack: Spice Cakes

Yields Provided: 12

Total Carbohydrates: 3 grams

Ingredients for Prep:

- Eggs (4)
- Baking powder (2 tsp.)
- Almond flour (2 cups)
- Salted butter (.5 cup)
- Nutmeg (.5 tsp.)
- Allspice (.5 tsp.)
- Ginger (.5 tsp.)
- Cinnamon (.5 tsp.)
- Erythritol (.75 cup)
- Ground cloves (.25 tsp.)
- Vanilla extract (1 tsp.)
- Water (5 tbsp.)

Method of Prep:
1. Set the temperature in the oven to 350° Fahrenheit. Prepare a cupcake tray with liners (12).
2. Mix the butter and erythritol with a hand mixer. Once it's smooth, combine with two eggs and the vanilla. Mix and stir in the remainder of the eggs, stirring until creamy.
3. Grind the clove to a fine powder and add with the rest of the spices. Whisk into the mixture. Stir in the baking powder and almond flour. Blend in the water. When the batter is smooth, add to the prepared tin.
4. Bake for 15 minutes. Enjoy any time.

Tips for Meal Prep:
1. Cool thoroughly for the prep.
2. It's recommended to place them in the refrigerator for a few days or in the freezer to enjoy later.

Day 7

Breakfast: Morning Hot Pockets

Yields Provided: 2

Total Carbohydrates: 4 grams

Ingredients for Prep:

- Shredded mozzarella - not fresh (.75 cup)
- Almond flour (.33 cup)
- Scrambled eggs (2 large)
- Ghee or unsalted butter (2 tbsp.)
- Slices of bacon (3 cooked)

Method of Prep:

1. Cook the bacon and eggs. Prepare the dough by melting the shredded mozzarella (stovetop @ low heat or in a microwave). Fold in the almond flour. Stir until the dough is well-combined.
2. Arrange the bacon strips in a large pan. Add two to three tablespoons of water. Steam-fry using the med-high heat setting until the water starts to boil.
3. Lower the temperature setting to medium. Simmer until the water evaporates and bacon fat is rendered. Reduce the temperature setting to low. Continue cooking until the bacon is crispy.
4. Grease the same skillet with half of the butter/ghee and add both eggs. Simmer using the med-low temperature until done, stirring continuously. Transfer to the countertop and add the rest of the butter.
5. Roll the dough out between two sheets of parchment paper (A silicone mat and silicone rolling pin are useful).
6. Place the bacon slices and scrambled eggs along the center.
7. Fold over and seal the dough. Make several holes for releasing the steam while baking.

8. Set the oven temperature to 400° Fahrenheit. Bake for about 20 minutes, or it is firm to the touch.

Tips for Meal Prep:
1. Transfer the hot pockets from the oven and let them cool.
2. Wrap in foil and toss into a freezer bag. Place on a baking tin to freeze solid.
3. *Note*: It is advisable to not leave in the refrigerator for storage.

Lunch: Greek Salad

Yields Provided: 1

Total Carbohydrates: 8 grams

Ingredients for Prep:
- Red onion (.25 cup)
- Tomato (.25 cup)
- Cucumber (.25 cup)
- Bell pepper (.25 cup)
- Feta cheese (.5 cup)
- Olive oil (3 tbsp.)
- Olives (1 tbsp.)
- Red wine vinegar (.5 tbsp.)

Method of Prep:
1. Dice the tomato, chop the olives, and slice the onion, cucumber, and pepper.
2. Combine the bell pepper, tomato, cucumber, crumbled feta cheese, and onion.

Tips for Meal Prep:

1. You can prepare the salad and pop into the fridge until time to eat.
2. Spritz using the oil and vinegar with a shake of salt and black pepper to your liking.
3. Toss until all of the ingredients are well mixed before serving.

Dinner: Buffalo Sloppy Joes

Yields Provided: 8

Total Carbohydrates: 2 grams

Ingredients for Prep:
- Coconut oil (1 tbsp.)
- Celery stalk (1 medium)
- Baby carrots (.25 cup)
- White onion (1 small)
- Garlic powder (1 tsp.)
- Red hot sauce (.5 cup)
- Mayonnaise (.25 cup)
- Ground chicken or turkey (1 lb.)

Method of Prep:
1. Pulse the baby carrots, celery stalk, and onion using a food processor. (You can also finely chop the veggies.)
2. Heat a skillet using the med-high temperature setting.
3. Pour in the coconut oil to heat. Toss in the minced veggies. Sauté for five to eight minutes. When it's ready, the carrots and onions will be fork tender.
4. Fold in the ground chicken. Continue to sauté until the chicken is thoroughly cooked.
5. Adjust the heat setting to low. Stir in the hot sauce and garlic powder.
6. Simmer for another five minutes. Remove from the burner.

Tips for Meal Prep:
1. Cool the chicken completely. Add to eight containers or freezer bags.
2. Store in the freezer until needed.
3. Defrost the portions needed to thaw.
4. Once it's dinner time, stir in the mayonnaise.
5. Note: Be sure the mixture is cool, or mayonnaise could curdle.
6. Spoon into your wrap or bun to serve.

Snack: Brownie Muffins

Yields Provided: 6

Total Carbohydrates: 4.4 grams

Ingredients for Prep:

- Salt (.5 tsp.)
- Flaxseed meal (1 cup)
- Cocoa powder (.25 cup)
- Cinnamon (1 tbsp.)
- Baking powder (.5 tbsp.)
- Coconut oil (2 tbsp.)
- Large egg (1)
- Vanilla extract (1 tsp.)
- Pumpkin puree (.5 cup)
- Sugar-free caramel syrup (.25 cup)
- Slivered almonds (.5 cup)
- Apple cider vinegar (1 tsp.)

Method of Prep:
1. Set the oven temperature to 350° Fahrenheit.
2. Use a deep mixing container—mix all of the fixings and stir well
3. Use six paper liners in the muffin tin, and add ¼ cup of batter to each one.
4. Sprinkle several almonds on the tops, pressing gently.
5. Bake approximately 15 minutes or when the top is set.

Tips for Meal Prep:
1. Cut the brownies into six portions.
2. Store in plastic baggies for the fridge or freezer bags if you want to have them last longer than three to four days.

Week 2

Day 8

Breakfast: Avocado Eggs

Yields Provided: 2

Total Carbohydrates: 9 grams

Ingredients for Prep:

- Eggs (2)
- Avocado (1 ripened)
- Black pepper and salt (to your liking)
- Optional: Hot sauce

Method of Prep:
1. Warm up the oven until it reaches 425° Fahrenheit.
2. Slice the avocado in half and discard the pit. Use a metal scoop to remove about one to two tablespoons of the fleshy insides.
3. Arrange the halves in a small baking pan. Crack an egg into both halves and season with some pepper and salt.
4. Bake for 15-20 minutes.

Tips for Meal Prep:
1. Let the fixings cool and store for a day or so in the refrigerator to enjoy the next morning or for a snack.
2. If you want to spice it up a little, sprinkle in a portion of keto-friendly hot sauce on the second day.

Lunch: Tuna Salad

Yields Provided: 2

Total Carbohydrates: 6 grams

Ingredients for Prep:

- Fresh lemon juice (half of 1)
- Olive oil (1 tbsp.)
- Large chopped boiled eggs (2)
- Tuna packed in oil (2 cans - 15 oz. each)
- Cucumber (half of 1)
- Medium red onions (2)
- Cilantro (half of 1)
- Salt (1 tsp.)
- Mayonnaise (2 tbsp.)
- Dijon mustard (2 tsp.)

Method of Prep:

1. Whisk the oil, lemon juice, mayo, and mustard in a container.
2. Thinly slice the cucumber and onions.
3. Drain the tuna and combine it with the remainder of the ingredients in another bowl.
4. Place each container in the fridge.

Tips for Meal Prep:

1. Add the dressing to the salad and toss to serve.

Dinner: Bacon & Shrimp Risotto

Yields Provided: 2

Total Carbohydrates: 5 grams

Ingredients for Prep:

- Bacon (4 slices)
- Daikon winter radish (2 cups)
- Dry white wine (2 tbsp.)
- Chicken stock (.25 cup)
- Garlic (1 clove)
- Ground pepper (as desired)
- Chopped parsley (2 tbsp.)
- Cooked shrimp (4 oz.)

Method of Prep:

1. Peel and slice the radish, mince the garlic, and chop the bacon. Remove as much water as possible from the daikon once it's shredded.
2. On the stovetop, heat up a saucepan using the medium heat temperature setting. Toss in the bacon and fry until it's crispy. Leave the drippings in the pan and remove the bacon with a slotted spoon to drain.
3. Add the stock, wine, daikon, salt, pepper, and garlic into the pan. Simmer for 6-8 minutes until most of the liquid is absorbed.
4. Fold in the bacon (saving a few bits for the topping), and shrimp along with the parsley. Serve.
5. *Tip*: If you cannot find the daikon, just substitute it using shredded cauliflower.

Tips for Meal Prep:

1. This delicious treat can be cooled and stored in the fridge for a day or two.
2. Save the bacon and shrimp in separate containers until ready to serve.

Snack: Pumpkin Pie Cupcakes

Yields Provided: 6

Total Carbohydrates: 2.9 grams

Ingredients for Prep:

- Coconut flour (3 tbsp.)
- Baking powder (.25 tsp.)
- Salt (1 pinch)
- Baking soda (.25 tsp.)
- Pumpkin pie spice (1 tsp.)
- Large egg (1)
- Pumpkin puree (.75 cup)
- Swerve Granular/Swerve Brown (.33 cup)
- Heavy whipping cream (.25 cup)
- Vanilla (.5 tsp.)

Method of Prep:

1. Warm up the oven to 350° Fahrenheit. Prepare the baking pan.
2. Whisk the coconut flour with the baking powder, pumpkin pie spice, baking soda, and salt.
3. In another container, whisk the pumpkin puree with the cream, sweetener, vanilla, and egg until well combined.
4. Whisk in the dry fixings. If the batter is too thin, whisk in an additional tablespoon of the coconut flour.
5. Portion into the muffin tins. Bake until puffed and barely set (25 to 30 min.).
6. Transfer the pan to the countertop (in the pan) to cool. Store in the fridge for a minimum of one hour before it's time to serve.
7. Top it off using a generous helping of whipped cream.
8. Note: They will sink when you let them cook. It will be that much tastier with the serving of whipped cream!

Tips for Meal Prep:

1. After they are cooled, store in the fridge until you want one to eat.
2. Top it off using the whipped cream.

Day 9

Breakfast: Tomato & Cheese Frittata

Yields Provided: 2

Total Carbohydrates: 6 grams

Ingredients for Prep:

- Eggs (6)
- Soft cheese (3.5 oz./.66 cup)
- White onion (half of 1 medium)
- Halved cherry tomatoes (.66 cup)
- Chopped herbs - ex. Chives or basil (2 tbsp.)
- Ghee/butter (1 tbsp.)

Method of Prep:
1. Set the oven broiler temperature to 400° Fahrenheit.
2. Arrange the onions on a greased - hot iron skillet. Cook with either ghee or butter until lightly browned.
3. In another dish, crack the eggs and flavor with salt, pepper, or add some herbs of your choice. Whisk and add to the pan of onions, cooking until the edges begin to get crispy.
4. Top with cheese (such as feta), and a few diced tomatoes. Put the pan in the broiler for five to seven minutes or until done.
5. Enjoy piping hot or let cool down.
6. Note: You can purge all of the leftover veggies into the recipe (if you wish).

Tips for Meal Prep:
1. Divide into two equal portions. Place in separate containers until you're ready to enjoy a healthy breakfast.
2. Enjoy this readily prepared frittata that you can serve either hot or cold.
3. The deliciously prepared frittata will remain good to serve for up to five days. So, prep enough for several days.

Lunch: Beef & Pepperoni Pizza

Yields Provided: 4

Total Carbohydrates: 2 grams

Ingredients for Prep:

- Large eggs (2)
- Ground beef (20 oz.)
- Pepperoni slices (28)
- Pizza sauce (.5 cup)
- Shredded cheddar cheese (.5 cup)
- Mozzarella cheese (4 oz.)
- Also Needed: 1 Cast iron skillet

Method of Prep:

1. Combine the eggs, beef, and seasonings and place in the skillet to form the crust. Bake until the meat is done or about 15 minutes.
2. Take it out of the oven and add the sauce, cheese, and toppings. Place the pizza back in the oven for a few more minutes until the cheese has melted.

Tips for Meal Prep:

1. After it's cooled completely, slice the pizza into four equal portions for freezing.
2. You can also leave it whole and freeze. Add it to a freezer bag until it's time to serve and enjoy.

Dinner: Chicken & Green Beans

Yields Provided: 3

Total Carbohydrates: 4 grams

Ingredients for Prep:

- Olive oil (2 tbsp.)
- Trimmed green beans (1 cup)
- Whole chicken breasts (2)
- Halved cherry tomatoes (8)
- Italian seasoning (1 tbsp.)
- Salt and pepper (1 tsp.)

Method of Prep:

1. Heat a skillet using the medium heat temperature setting. Pour in the oil.
2. Sprinkle the chicken with pepper, salt, and Italian seasoning.
3. Arrange in the skillet and fry for 10 minutes on each side or until well done.

Tips for Meal Prep:

1. Let the chicken cool. Place in a container until it's time to use.
2. Add the tomatoes and beans. Simmer another 5 to 7 minutes and serve.

Snack: Amaretti Cookies

Yields Provided: 16

Total Carbohydrates: 1 gram

Ingredients for Prep:

- Coconut flour (2 tbsp.)
- Cinnamon (.25 tsp.)
- Salt (.5 tsp.)
- Erythritol (.5 cup)
- Baking powder (.5 tsp.)
- Almond flour (1 cup)
- Eggs (2)
- Almond extract (.5 tsp.)
- Vanilla extract (.5 tsp.)
- Coconut oil (4 tbsp.)
- Sugar-free jam (2 tbsp.)
- Shredded coconut (1 tbsp.)

Method of Prep:
1. Cover the tin with a sheet of paper.
2. Warm up the oven to reach 400° Fahrenheit.
3. Sift the flour and combine all of the dry fixings.
4. After combined, work in the wet ones. Shape into 16 cookies.
5. Make a dent in the center of each one. Bake for 15 to 17 minutes

Tips for Meal Prep:
1. It is important to let them cool for a few minutes.
2. Add a dab of jam to each one and a sprinkle of coconut bits.

Day 10

Breakfast: Blueberry Pancake Bites

Yields Provided: 24 bites

Total Carbohydrates: 7.5 grams

Ingredients for Prep:

- Baking powder (1 tsp.)
- Water (.33 - .5 cup)
- Melted ghee (.25 cup)
- Coconut flour (.5 cup)
- Cinnamon (.5 tsp.)
- Salt (.5 tsp.)
- Eggs (4)
- Vanilla extract (.5 tsp.)
- Frozen blueberries (.5 cup)
- Also Needed: Muffin tray

Method of Prep:

1. Set the oven to reach 325° Fahrenheit. Use a spritz of coconut oil spray to grease 24 regular-sized muffin cups.
2. Combine the eggs, sweetener, and vanilla, mixing until well incorporated. Fold in the flour, melted ghee, baking powder, salt, and cinnamon. Stir in .33 cup of water to finish the batter.
3. The mixture should be thick. Next, divide the batter into the prepared cups with several berries in each one.
4. Bake until set (20 to 25 min.). Cool.

Tips for Meal Prep:

1. Store in an airtight container; preferable cool also.
2. It will be good for 8 to 10 days.
3. Freeze for 60 to 80 days.

Lunch: Buffalo Chicken Burgers

Yields Provided: 2 burgers

Total Carbohydrates: 1 gram

Ingredients for Prep:

- Chicken breasts (8 oz. cooked)
- Unchilled cream cheese (2 oz.)
- Shredded mozzarella cheese (.5 cup)
- Frank's Red-Hot Sauce or your preference (2 tbsp.)
- Coconut oil or ghee - for frying

Method of Prep:
1. Either chop or shred the prepared chicken and combine it with the rest of the fixings.
2. Place the fixings in the microwave for 15 to 20 seconds to help compact the ingredients. Form two medium patties and place them on a plate. Store in the freezer for about 15 minutes.
3. Heat a skillet using the high-temperature setting. Add the fat and patties. Prepare the burgers for 2 to 3 minutes per side.
4. Serve when crispy brown.

Tips for Meal Prep:
1. Prepare the chicken and mix to form patties.
2. Freeze, or cook and freeze the patties.

Dinner: Roasted Leg of Lamb

Yields Provided: 2

Total Carbohydrates: 1 gram

Ingredients for Prep:

- Reduced-sodium beef broth (.5 cup)
- Leg of lamb (2 lb.)
- Chopped garlic cloves (6)
- Fresh rosemary leaves (1 tbsp.)
- Black pepper (1 tsp.)
- Salt (2 tsp.)

Method of Prep:

1. Grease a baking pan and set the oven temperature to 400° Fahrenheit.
2. Arrange the lamb in the pan and add the broth and seasonings.
3. Roast 30 minutes and lower the heat to 350° Fahrenheit. Continue cooking for about one hour or until done.
4. Let the lamb stand about 20 minutes before slicing to serve.
5. Enjoy with some roasted brussels sprouts and extra rosemary for a tasty change of pace.

Tips for Meal Prep:

1. Cool and wrap any leftovers to use later.
2. Wrap well in plastic wrap and store in a freezer bag.

Day 11

Breakfast: Blueberry Essence

Yields Provided: 1

Total Carbohydrates: 3 grams

Ingredients for Prep:

- Blueberries (.25 cup)
- Coconut milk (1 cup)
- Optional: Whey protein powder (1 scoop)
- Vanilla Essence (1 tsp.)
- MCT Oil (1 tsp.)

Method of Prep:
1. For a quick burst of energy, add all of the fixings into a blender.
2. Puree until it reaches the desired consistency.

Tips for Meal Prep:
1. Store in the fridge until ready to enjoy.
2. Add several chunks of ice if you like.

Lunch: Italian Tomato Salad

Yields Provided: 2

Total Carbohydrates: 6 grams

Ingredients for Prep:

- Minced garlic clove (1)
- Freshly chopped basil (.25 cup)
- Balsamic vinegar (1 tbsp.)
- Olive oil (2 tbsp.)
- Pepper and salt (as desired)
- Sliced ripe tomatoes (2 medium)
- Fresh arugula (2 cups)
- Cubed mozzarella cheese (3 oz.)

Method of Prep:

1. Combine the oil, vinegar, basil, garlic, black pepper, and salt into a blender. Mix until it's creamy smooth.
2. Toss the rest of the fixings in a salad container.

Tips for Meal Prep:

1. Combine the salad and add the dressing mixture or add it to individual containers for an on-to-go method.
2. You can store this way for up to one day.

Dinner: Bacon Cheeseburger

Yields Provided: 12

Total Carbohydrates: 0.8 gram

Ingredients for Prep:

- Low-sodium bacon (16 oz. pkg.)
- Ground beef (3 lb.)
- Eggs (2)
- Medium chopped onion (half of 1)
- Shredded cheddar cheese (8 oz.)

Method of Prep:
1. Fry the bacon and chop to bits. Shred the cheese and dice the onion.
2. Combine the mixture with the beef and blend in the whisked eggs.
3. Prepare 24 burgers and grill them the way you like them. You can make a double-decker since they are small. If you like a larger burger, you can just make 12 burgers as a single-decker.

Tips for Meal Prep:
1. Let the cooked burgers cool.
2. Separate them into freezer bags for later use anytime you need a quick meal or snack.

Snack: Strawberry Cream Cheese Bites

Yields Provided: 12

Total Carbohydrates: 2 grams

Ingredients for Prep:

- Diced strawberries (1 cup)
- Vanilla extract (1 tsp.)
- Coconut oil (.25 cup)
- Unchilled cream cheese (.75 cup)
- Also Needed: 12-count muffin cup tin

Method of Prep:

1. Prepare a muffin tray with liners or grease with a spritz of cooking oil spray.
2. Toss the berries into the blender and mix until pureed.
3. Add in the rest of the fixings and mix until it's all smooth.
4. Scoop into the cups and freeze until solid (2 hrs.).

Tips for Meal Prep:

1. After they are frozen, your job is done.
2. Pop them out and store them in a freezer bag and enjoy any time you desire!

Day 12

Breakfast: Pancakes & Nuts

Yields Provided: 2

Total Carbohydrates: 9 grams

Ingredients for Prep:

- Almond flour (10 tbsp.)
- Baking soda (.5 tsp.)
- Ground cinnamon (1 tsp.)
- Large eggs (3)
- Almond milk (.25 cup)
- Chopped nuts – ex. Hazelnuts (.25 cup)
- Unsweetened almond/preference nut butter (.25 cup)

Method of Prep:

1. Whisk all of the fixings in a container. Let the batter sit for 5-10 minutes so the flour will thicken.
2. Warm-up a greased skillet (low-medium).
3. Measure out .25 cup portions of the batter in the frying pan. Cook for two to three minutes per side.

Tips for Meal Prep:

1. Let the pancakes cool.
2. Pour the nuts into a baggie or plastic container. You can add the nuts in the containers together or separately.
3. You can store the pancakes for 5-7 days in the refrigerator.
4. *Time to Eat*: Heat the pancakes and serve with the prepared almond butter drizzle.

Lunch: Pulled Pork for Sandwiches

Yields Provided: 8

Total Carbohydrates: 2.2 grams

Ingredients for Prep:

- Boneless pork shoulder (3 lb.)
- Chopped white onion (1)
- Bay leaves (3)
- Smoked paprika (1 tsp.)
- Garlic powder (2 tsp.)
- Pink Himalayan salt (3 tsp.)

Method of Prep:
1. Warm a slow cooker using the low setting. Combine the paprika, salt, and garlic powder. Slice the pork into chunks and rub into the spices.
2. Chop the onion and toss it into the cooker along with the pork.
3. Add the bay leaves and close the lid. Cook for 10 hours on low.
4. When ready, shred, and let cool.

Tips for Meal Prep:
1. Add the shredded pork to individual bags for the freezer or into compartmentalized dishes to await a veggie.
2. Be sure to date the containers and label with the name of its content.

Dinner: Shrimp Alfredo

Yields Provided: 4

Total Carbohydrates: 6.5 grams

Ingredients for Prep:

- Raw shrimp (1 lb.)
- Salted butter (1 tbsp.)
- Cubed cream cheese (4 oz.)
- Whole milk (.5 cup)
- Salt (1 tsp.)
- Garlic powder (1 tbsp.)
- Dried basil (1 tsp.)
- Shredded parmesan cheese (.5 cup)
- Baby kale or spinach (.25 cup)
- Whole sun-dried tomatoes (5)

Method of Prep:

1. Warm the butter using the medium heat temperature setting in a skillet.
2. Toss in the shrimp and lower the heat to med-low. After 30 seconds, flip the shrimp and cook until slightly pink. Blend in the cream cheese.
3. Increase the heat and pour in the milk. Stir frequently.
4. Sprinkle with the salt, basil, and garlic. Empty the parmesan cheese in and mix well.
5. Simmer until the sauce has thickened. Cut the sun-dried tomatoes into strips.
6. Lastly, fold in the kale/spinach and dried tomatoes. Serve steaming hot.

Tips for Meal Prep:

1. Cool thoroughly and store in the fridge to enjoy in a day or two

Snack: Coconut Macaroons

Yields Provided: 40 cookies/20 servings

Total Carbohydrates: 1 gram

Ingredients for Prep:

- Water (.33 cup)
- Low carb sweetener (.75 cup or less to taste)
- Sea salt (.25 tsp.)
- Sugar-free vanilla extract (.75 tsp.)
- Large eggs (2)
- Unsweetened shredded coconut (3-4 cups)
- *Optional*: Sugar-free chocolate chips
- Nonstick cooking oil spray

Method of Prep:

1. Set the oven to reach 350° Fahrenheit.
2. Lightly spray the cookie tin with the oil spray.
3. Combine the sweetener, water, vanilla extract, and salt in the pan.
4. Bring to a boil using the med-high temperature setting. Stir well and remove from the burner.
5. Combine the coconut flakes and egg in a food processor. Pour in the syrup and pulse. Scoop the dough onto the prepared cookie tin (one-inch apart).
6. Bake for eight minutes, rotating the cookie tin in the oven.
7. Continue baking until lightly browned or approximately four additional minutes.
8. Cool on the rack. Garnish with the melted chocolate as desired.

Tips for Meal Prep:

1. Note: Start with 3 cups of dried coconut shredded coconut.
2. You can add more as needed for the desired consistency, depending on taste preference.
3. After they are cooled, melt the chocolate, and serve.

Day 13

Breakfast: Cinnamon Smoothie

Yields Provided: 1

Total Carbohydrates: 5 grams

Ingredients for Prep:

- Cinnamon (.5 tsp.)
- Coconut milk (.5 cup)
- Water (.5 cup)
- Extra-virgin coconut oil/MCT oil (1 tbsp.)
- Ground chia seeds (1 tbsp.)
- Plain/vanilla whey protein (.25 cup)
- Optional: Stevia drops

Method of Prep:

1. Pour the milk, cinnamon, protein powder, and chia seeds in a blender.
2. Empty the coconut oil, ice, and water. Add a few drops of stevia to your liking.

Tips for Meal Prep:

1. Store in the fridge until ready to enjoy.
2. Add several chunks of ice if you like.

Lunch: Pita Pizza

Yields Provided: 2

Ingredients for Prep:

- Marinara sauce (.5 cup)
- Low-carb pita (1)
- Cheddar cheese (2 oz.)
- Pepperoni (14 slices)
- Roasted red peppers (1 oz.)

Method of Prep:

1. Set the oven to 450° Fahrenheit.
2. Slice the pita in half and put on a foil-lined baking tray. Rub with a bit of oil and toast for one to two minutes.
3. Pour the sauce over the bread, sprinkle with the cheese, and other toppings. Bake for an additional five minutes or until the cheese melts.

Tips for Meal Prep:

1. Remove the pizza from the oven and cool it thoroughly.
2. Store in the fridge for a couple of days.
3. Freeze to enjoy later using a freezer bag.

Dinner: Roasted Chicken & Tomatoes

Yields Provided: 2

Total Carbohydrates: 5 grams

Ingredients for Prep:

- Olive oil (1 tbsp.)
- Plum tomatoes (2 quartered)
- Chicken legs – bone-in with skin (2)
- Paprika (1 tsp.)
- Ground oregano (1 tsp.)
- Balsamic vinegar (1 tbsp.)

Method of Prep:

1. Set the oven temperature setting at 350° Fahrenheit. Grease a roasting pan with a spritz of oil.
2. Rinse and lightly dab the chicken legs dry with a paper towel. Prepare using the oil and vinegar over the skin. Season with the paprika and oregano.
3. Arrange the legs in the pan along with the tomatoes around the edges.
4. Cover with a layer of foil and bake one hour. Baste to prevent the chicken from drying out.
5. Discard the foil and increase the temperature to 425° Fahrenheit.
6. Bake 15 to 30 minutes more until browned and the juices run clear.
7. Serve with a side salad.

Tips for Meal Prep:

1. If you plan to use this for meal prep only, stop at step 4. Put in a zipper-type freezer bag.
2. Freeze the contents until another time. Proceed by baking.

Snack: Pecan Turtle Truffles

Yields Provided: 15

Total Carbohydrates: 1

Ingredients for Prep:

- Swerve or your preference (.33 cup)
- Melted butter (.5 cup)
- Vanilla extract (.25 tsp.)
- Caramel extract (.5 tsp.)
- Vanilla protein powder -0- carbs (.33 cup)
- Finely ground pecans (1 cup)
- 85% chocolate - Lindt or your choice (4 squares)
- Pecan halves (15)

Method of Prep:

1. Combine the sweetener, butter, vanilla extract, caramel extracts, finely ground pecans and protein powder in a mixing container.
2. Roll into 15 truffles and place them on a sheet of parchment or waxed paper.
3. Melt the chocolate in a baggie in the microwave for one minute. Snip the corner and squeeze the chocolate over the prepared truffles.
4. Garnish each truffle with a pecan half. Chill and enjoy any time.

Tips for Meal Prep:

1. Store in the fridge for the truffles to remain fresh.

Day 14

Breakfast: Bacon Cheese & Egg Cups

Yields Provided: 6

Total Carbohydrates: 1 gram

Ingredients for Prep:

- Large eggs (6)
- Bacon (6 strips)
- Cheese (.25 cup)
- Fresh spinach (1 handful)
- Pepper & Salt (as desired)

Method of Prep:

1. Warm up the oven to 400° Fahrenheit.
2. Prepare the bacon using medium heat on the stovetop. Place on towels to drain.
3. Grease 6 muffin tins with a spritz of oil.
4. Line each tin with a slice of bacon, pressing tightly to make a secure well for the eggs.
5. Drain and dry the spinach with a paper towel. Whisk the eggs and combine with the spinach.
6. Add the mixture to the prepared tins and sprinkle with cheese. Sprinkle with salt and pepper until it's like you like it.
7. Bake for 15 minutes. Remove when done and cool.

Tips for Meal Prep:

1. Prepare the cups and store them in airtight containers.
2. Reheat when ready to eat. It keeps in the fridge for 3-4 days.

Lunch: Caprese Salad

Yields Provided: 4

Total Carbohydrates: 5 grams

Ingredients for Prep:

- Grape tomatoes (3 cups)
- Peeled garlic cloves (4)
- Avocado oil (2 tbsp.)
- Mozzarella balls (19 pearl-sized)
- Fresh basil leaves (.25 cup)
- Baby spinach leaves (4 cups)
- Brine reserved from the cheese (1 tbsp.)
- Pesto (1 tbsp.)

Method of Prep:

1. Use a sheet of aluminum foil to cover a baking tray.
2. Set the oven temperature at 400° Fahrenheit.
3. Arrange the cloves and tomatoes on the baking pan. Drizzle with oil. Bake for 20 to 30 minutes until the tops are lightly browned.
4. Drain the liquid (saving one tablespoon) from the mozzarella. Mix the pesto with the brine.
5. Arrange the spinach in a large serving bowl. Transfer the tomatoes to the dish along with the roasted garlic.

Tips for Meal Prep:

1. Cool the ingredients thoroughly. Place in closed containers until time to use.
2. Drizzle with the pesto sauce. Garnish with the mozzarella balls and freshly torn basil leaves.

Dinner: Enchilada Skillet Dinner

Yields Provided: 4

Total Carbohydrates: 7 grams

Ingredients for Prep:

- Small yellow onion (1)
- Ground beef (1.5 lb.)
- Red enchilada sauce (.66 cup)
- Chopped green onions (8)
- Diced Roma tomatoes (2)
- Shredded cheddar cheese (4 oz.)
- Optional: Freshly chopped cilantro (as desired)

Method of Prep:

1. Use a wok or skillet to sauté the yellow onion and meat. Drain the juices and add the green onions, tomato, and enchilada sauce.
2. Once it starts to boil, simmer for about 5 minutes. Sprinkle with the salt and cheese. Continue cooking until the cheese has melted.
3. Stir in the cilantro. Serve over chopped lettuce and serving of sour cream. Add the extra carbs and enjoy.

Tips for Meal Prep:

1. If you have any leftovers, omit the cilantro, lettuce, and sour cream.
2. Wrap each portion tightly in plastic wrap and then in foil. Freeze.
3. Remove from the freezer and bake at 350° Fahrenheit until the cheese is melted, and the dinner is warmed.

Chapter 5:
Meal Prep for Kids

You will find these quick and easy recipes are easy to prepare in a short time!

Special Smoothie Options: Smoothies are included for children who don't always like veggies or some fruits. All that is required is a freezer-safe container or a push-up popsicle mold to make a special snack.

You can make a unique pack using 2 cups of fruit, 1 cup of optional greens, and a sliced banana. When you're ready to eat, place 1 cup of liquid into the blender (or half yogurt and half water), add the fruit, and mix. Day 2 and 4 are using the mango base with additional boosters to make it a meal.

Week 1

Day 1

Breakfast: Apple Banana Muffins

Yields Provided: 12

Ingredients for Prep:

- Baking powder (1 tsp.)
- Whole wheat flour (1.33 cups)
- Salt (.25 tsp.)
- Baking soda (.5 tsp.)
- Egg (1)
- Olive oil (3 tbsp.)
- Unsweetened applesauce (.5 cup)
- Vanilla extract (1 tsp.)
- Ripe bananas (1.5 cups)

Method of Prep:

1. Set the oven temperature at 375° Fahrenheit.
2. Heavily grease a muffin tin.
3. Whisk the egg and mashed bananas. Fold in everything except the flour.
4. Lastly, stir in the flour, using caution not to overmix.
5. Portion the batter into each of the tins.
6. Bake for approximately 20-25 minutes.

Tips for Meal Prep:

1. When the muffins are done, transfer them to the countertop leaving them in the pan for about five minutes. Arrange them on a cooling rack to thoroughly cool before proceeding.

2. Place the muffins into a freezer bag or another type of storage container.
3. Store in the fridge for about five days or freeze for later.

Lunch: Cranberry Tuna Salad

Yields Provided: 5

Ingredients for Prep:

- White tuna - packed in water (16 oz. can)
- Low-fat mayo (3 tbsp.)
- Salt and pepper (as desired)
- Light sour cream (3 tbsp.)
- Celery (.5 cup)
- Red onion (.25 cup)
- Lemon juice (1 tbsp.)
- Dried cranberries (.25 cup)
- Apple (1 diced)

Method of Prep:
1. Drain the tuna.
2. Chop the celery and mince the onion. Measure out the rest of the fixings.
3. Combine and mix all of the ingredients.

Tips for Meal Prep:
1. Place a cover on the salad.
2. Store in the refrigerator to enjoy for breakfast or brunch.

Dinner: Hawaiian Chicken Kebabs

Yields Provided: 8

Ingredients for Prep:

- Chicken breasts (1 lb.)
- Yellow & Red bell pepper (half of 1 each)
- Purple or red onion (half of 1)
- Pineapple chunks (1.5 cups)
- Pineapple (.5 cup)
- Orange (.5 cup)
- Teriyaki sauce (.25 cup)
- Salt (1 tsp.)
- Ginger (.5 tsp.)
- Onion powder (1 tsp.)
- Black pepper (1 tsp.)
- Garlic powder (1 tsp.)

Method of Prep:

1. Soak the wooden skewers in water for one hour.
2. Slice the peppers and onions into 1-inch pieces.
3. Prepare the marinade (orange juice, teriyaki, and pineapple) Marinate the chicken for one to two hours.
4. Prepare the skewers. Alternate the chicken and veggies (2 to 3 of each veggie and 3 to 4 pieces of meat).
5. Combine the spices in a small container (black pepper, salt ginger, onion, and garlic powder). Sprinkle over the kebabs.
6. Cook on the grill (med. flame) 5 to 6 minutes on each side.
7. Take the goodies from the skewers and enjoy the feast.

Tips for Meal Prep:

1. You have two options.
2. *Option 1:* Go through step 3 to prepare the skewers,
3. Cover the skewers with foil and cook the following day.
4. Continue the recipe.
5. *Option 2:* Prepare and cook the kebabs. Remove from the

skewers if desired.

6. Store in the fridge. For best results, enjoy the next day or two

Snack: Apple Pie Cookies

Yields Provided: 24

Ingredients for Prep:

- Sugar-free yellow cake mix (1 box)
- Applesauce - unsweetened (.5 cup)
- Eggs (2)
- Diced apples (1 cup)
- Cinnamon (.5 tsp.)

Method of Prep:

1. Warm the oven temperature at 375° Fahrenheit.
2. Prepare a baking tin with a silicone baking mat or a piece of parchment paper.
3. Combine all of the fixings, mixing well. Scoop out and make one-inch balls. Arrange in the pan about two inches apart.
4. Bake until they're done to your liking or about 10 to 12 minutes.

Tips for Meal Prep:

1. Prepare the cookies and let them cool.
2. Store in an airtight container until desired.

Day 2

Breakfast: Mango Smoothie Base & Oats

Yields Provided: 1

Ingredients for Prep:

- Frozen mango chunks (1.5 cups)
- Liquid: Coconut water, dairy milk, almond milk, or water (1 to 1.5 cups)
- Optional: Chia seeds (1 tbsp.)

Method of Prep:

1. Combine the fixings in a blender until creamy smooth.
2. Use these optional nutrient boosters as desired:
   a. Ground flax (1 tbsp.)
   b. Hemp seeds (1 tbsp.)
   c. Coconut oil (1 tbsp.)
   d. Avocado (¼ of 1)
   e. Goji berries (1 tbsp.)
3. Add .25 cup of oatmeal to finish the smoothie with the boosters and base.

Tips for Meal Prep:

1. Freeze the prepared smoothie.
2. The night before, you can place the container in the fridge to defrost.
3. You can also put it into a lunchbox with a straw to be defrosted for lunches or a quick treat.

Lunch: Buffalo Chicken Tenders

Yields Provided: 6

Ingredients for Prep:

- Chicken breasts (1 lb.)
- Panko breadcrumbs (1 cup)
- Flour (.25 cup)
- Eggs (3)
- Red hot sauce (.33 cup)
- Brown sugar (.5 cup)
- Garlic powder (.5 tsp.)
- Water (3 tbsp.)

Method of Prep:

1. Set the oven setting to 425° Fahrenheit. Lightly prepare a baking sheet with a spritz of cooking oil.
2. Slice the chicken into strips and pound into a ½-inch thickness for even cooking and tenderness. Toss into a zipper-type baggie along with the flour. Shake well.
3. Add the breadcrumbs in one dish and the eggs in another.
4. Place the sliced pieces of chicken in with the eggs, then the breadcrumbs. Arrange on the prepared pan. Lightly spray with a misting of cooking oil.
5. Bake 20 minutes.
6. Prepare the sauce with the rest of the fixings in a small saucepan.

Tips for Meal Prep:

1. Let the chicken strips and sauce cool completely.
2. Wrap the chicken and place it in an airtight container. Add the sauce to another dish and store both in the fridge.
3. When ready to eat, warm the fixings.
4. Prepare any veggies you want as a side dish.
5. Enjoy the tenders with the sauce and your favorite side of veggies.

Dinner: Chili & Mac 'n' Cheese

Yields Provided: 6

Ingredients for Prep:

- Cooked ground beef (.5 lb.)
- Box - your favorite Mac 'n' cheese (1)
- Red kidney beans (1 cup)
- Green, canned chili (1 can - 4 oz.)
- Grated cheddar cheese (.25 cup)
- Chili powder (2 tsp.)

Method of Prep:
1. Prepare the box of macaroni and cheese.
2. Cook the ground beef until done.
3. Combine all of the fixings and serve.

Tips for Meal Prep:
1. You can divide the leftovers into individual containers to use over the next few days or leave it in one bowl for the next dining meal.

Snack: Pumpkin Cupcakes

Yields Provided: 24

Ingredients for Prep:

- 100% Pumpkin puree (15 oz. can)
- Water (1 cup)
- Sugar-free yellow cake mix (1 box)
- Also Needed: 2 dozen muffin tins with liners

Method of Prep:

1. Set the oven temperature setting to 350° Fahrenheit.
2. Prepare the muffin tins.
3. Combine all of the fixings. Pour into the prepared cupcake holders
4. Bake until lightly browned or about 22 minutes.

Tips for Meal Prep:

1. Transfer the cupcakes to the countertop and cool on a rack.
2. When they are fully cooled, store in the fridge.
3. Freeze to use anytime.

Day 3

Breakfast: Banana Almond Pancakes

Yields Provided: 4

Ingredients for Prep:

- Banana (half of 1)
- Large egg (1)
- Cinnamon (.125 tsp.)
- Ground almond flour (1 tsp.)
- Olive oil (2 tbsp.)

Method of Prep:

1. Whisk the egg and mix with the cinnamon and flour.
2. Mash the banana using a fork and combine it with the rest of the fixings.
3. Warm the oil in a skillet. Pour the batter to the pan. Flip once during the cooking process.
4. You'll have delicious pancakes in 20 minutes from start to finish.

Tips for Meal Prep:

1. Cool thoroughly and store in freezer bags according to how many servings you will use at one time.
2. Place the frozen pancakes onto a microwave-safe dish.
3. Microwave using the high setting for 1- 1.5 minutes.
4. Garnish with your favorite toppings.

Lunch: Colored Iceberg Salad

Yields Provided: 4

Ingredients for Prep:

- Iceberg lettuce (1 head)
- Bacon (6 slices)
- Sliced green onions (2)
- Sliced radishes (6)
- Shredded carrots (3)
- Red vinegar (.25 cup)
- Minced cloves of garlic (3)
- Olive oil (.25 cup)
- Black pepper (1 pinch)

Method of Prep:

1. Prepare the bacon in a skillet until crispy. Arrange on paper towels to drain the grease.
2. Use a large-sized salad bowl or individual dishes to prepare the salad.
3. Combine the torn lettuce leaves with the black pepper, garlic, carrots, green onions, bacon, oil, vinegar, and radishes.

Tips for Meal Prep:

1. This is a great one for the kids to get healthy veggies by using delightful colors.
2. Cover with plastic lids or plastic wrap until time for lunch.

Dinner: Delicious Meatloaf

Yields Provided: 6

Ingredients for Prep:

- 93% lean ground beef (2 lb.)
- Almond flour (2 tbsp.)
- Coconut flour (2 tbsp.)
- Garlic powder (1 tsp.)
- Onion powder (1 tsp.)
- Black pepper (.25 tsp.)
- Salt (1 tsp.)
- Egg (1)
- Worcestershire sauce (1 tbsp.)
- Regular or almond milk (1 tbsp.)
- BARBECUE sauce (.5 cup + more for serving)
- Also Needed: 9x5 loaf pan

Method of Prep:

1. Warm the oven at 350° Fahrenheit. Prepare the pan in
2. Note: You can also place the loaf pan on a baking tray to prevent spillovers in the oven.
3. Whisk the salt, pepper, garlic powder, and both flours in a mixing container.
4. In another container, mix the egg, barbecue sauce, milk Worcestershire sauce, and ground beef.
5. Combine everything and place it in the pan.
6. Bake for 45-65 minutes (depending on its thickness).
7. After it has baked for about halfway (20 min.), add barbecue sauce to the top and continue baking until the internal temperature reaches 155 Fahrenheit.
8. Serve and prepare the rest for freezing.

Tips for Meal Prep:

1. Cool thoroughly and place in a storage container and freeze for another time.

Snack: Whole Grain Banana Bread

Yields Provided: 14

Ingredients for Prep:

- Millet flour (.5 cup)
- Quinoa flour (.5 cup)
- Rice flour (.5 cup)
- Tapioca flour (.5 cup)
- Amaranth flour - brown (.5 cup)
- Baking powder (.5 tsp.)
- Salt (.125 cup)
- Baking soda (1 tsp.)
- Grapeseed oil (2 tbsp.)
- Raw sugar (.5 cup)
- Mashed banana (2 cups)
- Egg whites (.75 cup)
- Also Needed: 1 loaf pan - 5 by 9-inch

Method of Prep:

1. Lightly spray the loaf pan with a spritz of cooking oil. Sprinkle with a little flour and set aside.
2. Heat the oven temperature setting to reach 350° Fahrenheit.
3. Combine each of the dry fixings in a large mixing container - omitting the sugar.
4. Whisk the egg, mashed banana, oil, and sugar in another bowl. Thoroughly mix, adding the fixings to the loaf pan.
5. Bake for 50-60 minutes.

Tips for Meal Prep:

1. Transfer the loaf pan to the countertop to cool.
2. When cooled, place the entire loaf in a freezer bag. You can also slice and store the bread in the fridge or freezer for individual servings.

Day 4

Breakfast: Mango Smoothie Base & Greens

Yields Provided: 1

Ingredients for Prep:

- Liquid: Almond milk, coconut water, dairy milk, or water (1 to 1.5 cups)
- Frozen mango chunks (1.5 cups)
- Optional: Chia seeds (1 tbsp.)

Method of Prep:

1. Combine the smoothie fixings in a blender until creamy.
2. Use these optional nutrient boosters as desired:
   a. Hemp seeds (1 tbsp.)
   b. Ground flax (1 tbsp.)
   c. Avocado (¼ of 1)
   d. Coconut oil (1 tbsp.)
   e. Goji berries (1 tbsp.)

Tips for Meal Prep:

1. Add a scoop of protein powder with the boosters and base to finish the smoothie. Jazz it up to suit your youngster.
2. Store the smoothie in the freezer.
3. The night before, place the container in the fridge to defrost.
4. You can also add it to a lunchbox with a straw to be defrosted for a quick treat.

Lunch: Tuna Melt

Yields Provided: 4

Ingredients for Prep:

- Chunk white tuna – packed in water (12 oz. can)
- Coleslaw – packaged or homemade (1.5 cups)
- Green onion chopped (3 tbsp.)
- Mayonnaise – fat-free (3 tbsp.)
- Dijon-style mustard (1 tbsp.)
- English muffins – split in half (4)
- Cheddar cheese, reduced-fat – shredded (.33 cup)

Method of Prep:

1. Warm up the barbecue grill, broiler, or toaster oven.
2. Mix the drained tuna, coleslaw, and onions.
3. Whisk the mayo and mustard. Mix well.
4. Stir in the tuna mixture and combine well.

Tips for Meal Prep:

1. Place a lid on the tuna dish and store it in the fridge.
2. When it's mealtime, cut the muffins into halves.
3. Spread the tuna mixture on the muffins and arrange on a broiler pan.
4. Place on the rack about four inches from the burner. Broil for 3-4 minutes.
5. Toss the cheese over the top to melt and broil for about one to two minutes.

Dinner: Loaded Bacon Mac & Cheese

Yields Provided: 4-6

Ingredients for Prep:

- Mac 'n' Cheese (1 box)
- Cooked bacon (1 cup)
- Grated Monterey Jack cheese (.25 cup)
- Grated mozzarella cheese (.25 cup)

Method of Prep:

1. Make the macaroni and cheese and prepare the bacon.
2. Combine all of the fixings to serve now.
3. Note: It is noted by some that the powdered cheese is not as tasty as the creamy options.

Tips for Meal Prep:

1. You can prepare the mac 'n' cheese and bacon but store them individually until time to serve or use.
2. It will not store well in the freezer but should be good for several days.

Snack: Banana Oatmeal Cookies

Yields Provided: 36 cookies

Ingredients for Prep:

- All-purpose flour (1.5 cups)
- Ground nutmeg (.25 tsp.)
- Salt (.25 tsp.)
- Baking soda (1 tsp.)
- Butter (.25 cup or .5 stick)
- Ripened mashed bananas (2-3 medium or 1 cup)
- Brown sugar - Firmly packed (1 cup)
- Egg (1 large)
- Applesauce (.5 cup)
- Vanilla (1 tsp.)
- Old-fashioned rolled oats (2.5 cups)
- *Optional:* Chopped nuts (1 cup)

Method of Prep:

1. Combine the nutmeg, salt, flour, and baking soda. Set aside for now.
2. Beat the butter and brown sugar in a large mixing container using the medium setting of an electric mixer until well blended.

Fold in and mix the vanilla, egg, applesauce, and mashed bananas.

3. Using the low-speed setting, combine with the flour until just combined. Stir in the oats and nuts. Mix until just incorporated.
4. Place the container in the fridge for 10 minutes or up to six hours.
5. When ready to bake, just warm up the oven to 350° Fahrenheit.
6. Prepare the baking pan with some cooking spray. (Tip: Bake on a parchment paper-lined pan or silicone liner for the best results.)
7. Spoon the dough onto the tins about three inches apart and bake 15 to 17 minutes. Remove while they're still soft on the top.
8. Let them rest in the pan a few minutes before moving with a spatula to a cooling rack.

Tips for Meal Prep:
1. Make this batch any time your snacks are getting low.
2. Once they are moved to the cooling rack; cool thoroughly.
3. Store in a closed container to use later.

Day 5

Breakfast: 2-Ingredient Pancakes

Yields Provided: 12-inch pancake (1)

Ingredients for Prep:

- Eggs (2)
- Ripe banana (1)
- Cinnamon
- Vanilla

Method of Prep:

1. Mash the bananas and whisk two eggs.
2. Use some cooking spray to grease the skillet/griddle. Scrape in the batter.
3. No syrup is needed for these tasty treats. Add a little cinnamon or vanilla if desired.

Tips for Meal Prep:

1. Prepare these deliciously quick and easy pancakes.
2. You can do this the night or day before you want them.
3. Either freeze or let it chill in the fridge for a day.

Lunch: Pear & Banana Breakfast Salad

Yields Provided: 2

Ingredients for Prep:

- Asian pear (1)
- Banana (1)
- Lime (half of 1)
- Cinnamon powder (5 tsp.)
- Toasted pepitas (2 oz.)

Method of Prep:

1. Core and cube the pear. Peel and slice the banana. Toast the pepitas. Juice the lime.
2. Combine all of the fixings into two dishes.

Tips for Meal Prep:

1. Store in the fridge until time to serve.
2. Toss well and serve it onto serving platters for breakfast.

Dinner: Chicken Fried Rice

Yields Provided: 6

Ingredients for Prep:

- Cooking oil spray (2 squirts)
- Scallions (.5 cup)
- Carrots (.5 cup)
- Frozen-thawed green peas (.5 cup)
- Cooked regular or instant long-grain brown rice (2 cups)
- Garlic cloves (2)
- Egg whites (4 large)
- Soy sauce - low-sodium (3 tbsp.)
- Chicken breasts (12 oz.- ½-inch cubes)

Method of Prep:

1. Chop the green and white parts of the scallion and dice the carrots and garlic. Remove all of the skin and bones from the chicken. Scramble or cook the egg to your liking for the mixture.
2. Prepare a skillet with the spray and set the temperature to med-high.
3. Toss in the garlic and scallions to sauté for two minutes.
4. Stir in the carrots and chicken and sauté about five more minutes.
5. Fold in the prepared brown rice, cooked egg whites, peas, and soy. Sauté for about one minute.
6. Let it cool entirely.

Tips for Meal Prep:

1. Your kids will love this.
2. Cooked chicken can stay in the fridge for 3-4 days. After that, you'll need to toss it. You can also freeze it for longer prep times.
3. *Option 1:* Heat the rice using the microwave. Add a few tablespoons of broth or water per one cup of rice. Cover to create a steaming effect as it reheats.

4. *Option 2:* Stir-fry the rice: Use a sauté pan or large wok to heat canola or peanut oil using the high-temperature setting.

Snack: Apples & Dip

Yields Provided: 4

Ingredients for Prep:
- Chopped peanuts (2 tbsp.)
- Unchilled fat-free cream cheese (8 oz.)
- Vanilla (1.5 tsp.)
- Brown sugar (2 tbsp.)
- Orange juice (.5 cup)
- Apples (8 small or 4 medium)

Method of Prep:
1. Chop the peanuts well and place them in a storage container.
2. Take the cream cheese out of the fridge for about 5 minutes to soften at room temperature.
3. Combine the cream cheese with vanilla and brown sugar until smooth.

Tips for Meal Prep:
1. Store the mixture in the fridge.
2. Time to Eat: Remove the core from the apples and slice.
3. Fold the nuts into the cream cheese mixture.
4. Serve the dip with sliced apples and a drizzle of juice on top.

Day 6

Breakfast: Mango Smoothie Base & Tofu

Yields Provided: 1

Ingredients for Prep:

- Frozen mango chunks (1.5 cups)
- Liquid: Dairy milk, almond milk, coconut water, or water (1 to 1.5 cups)
- Optional: Chia seeds (1 tbsp.)

Method of Prep:

1. Combine the fixings in a blender until smooth. Store in the freezer until time to use.
2. Use these optional nutrient boosters as desired
   a. Coconut oil (1 tbsp.)
   b. Hemp seeds (1 tbsp.)
   c. Avocado (¼ of 1)
   d. Goji berries (1 tbsp.)
   e. Ground flax (1 tbsp.)
3. Add 3 ounces of tofu to the chosen fixings and mix until it's the desired consistency.

Tips for Meal Prep:

1. Freeze the prepared smoothie in a freezer bag or freezer-safe jar.
2. The night before, you can put the container in the fridge to defrost.
3. Add the frozen smoothie into a lunchbox with a straw. It will defrost by lunchtime.

Lunch: Chicken Salad

Yields Provided: 6

Ingredients for Prep:

- Shredded chicken breast (2 cups)
- Mayonnaise (1 tbsp.)
- Nonfat sour cream (.25 cup)
- Nonfat Greek yogurt (.5 cup)
- Bell pepper (2 tbsp.)
- Gala apple (half of 1)
- Garlic powder (1 tsp.)
- Dill pickle relish (1 tsp.)
- Onion powder (1 tsp.)
- Freshly cracked black pepper (.5 tsp.)
- Paprika (.5 tsp.)
- Salt (.5 tsp.)

Method of Prep:
1. Combine all of the fixings with a sprinkle of the pepper and salt as desired.

Tips for Meal Prep:
1. Prepare the salad and store in the refrigerator using a glass container with a lid.
2. Serve it any time for a snack or lunch on your choice of bread, veggies, or crackers.

Dinner: Cheesy Beef Egg Rolls

Yields Provided: 8

Ingredients for Prep:

- Egg roll wrappers (8)
- Cheddar cheese stick - cut in half (4)
- Cooked roast beef - chopped (2 cups)
- Creamy style horseradish (.25 cup)
- Frying oil

Method of Prep:

1. Warm a deep fryer or oil in a pan to approximately 350° Fahrenheit. Prepare an egg roll wrapper, placed in a diamond shape.
2. Place a small amount of horseradish sauce in the center. Lay down ¼ cup of shredded beef. Arrange a cheese stick (half) over the beef and fold in the two sides. Take the bottom point and fold it like an envelope.
3. Wet the top side of the wrapper with water along the edge.
4. Roll from the bottom to form the stick into the shape of a cigar.

Tips for Meal Prep:

1. Cool and use within a day or so. You can also freeze and prepare later.
2. Bake for 12-15 minutes at 400° Fahrenheit.

Snack: Banana Roll-Ups

Yields Provided: 2

Ingredients for Prep:

- Whole wheat bread (1 slice)
- Medium peeled banana (.5 of 1)
- Salt-free chunky peanut butter (1.5 tsp.)

Method of Prep:

1. Use a rolling pin to flatten the bread.
2. Apply the peanut butter to one side of the bread. Add the banana.
3. Roll it up and slice into three to four segments.

Tips for Meal Prep:

1. After you roll up the bananas, just store them in the fridge in a closed container.
2. Enjoy anytime.

Day 7

Breakfast: Berry Monkey Bread Cinnamon Rolls

Yields Provided: 6

Ingredients for Prep:

- Refrigerated orange rolls (2 cans)
- Berries (2 pints)
- Optional: Softened cream cheese (3 oz.)
- Basil (3 tbsp.)

Method of Prep:
1. Chop the orange rolls and scatter them onto the bottom of a greased bundt pan.
2. Sprinkle with half of the berries, and repeat.
3. You can also press a dollop or two of cream cheese in the dough and berries with a sprinkle of basil.
4. Bake for 20 minutes. Wait a few minutes and turn it over and out.
5. Drizzle with the orange spread if you are using it the same day.

Tips for Meal Prep:
1. If these are for prep, wait on adding the spread until it's time to eat.
2. Leave the rinsed berries in a container also until mealtime.

Lunch: Strawberry Sandwiches

Yields Provided: 4

Ingredients for Prep:

- Stevia or favorite sweetener (1 tbsp.)
- Softened cream cheese - low-fat (8 oz.)
- Grated lemon zest (1 tsp.)
- Whole wheat English muffins (4 toasted)
- Sliced strawberries (2 cups)

Method of Prep:

1. Slice the strawberries. Set the low-fat cheese out to soften. Grate the lemon.
2. Use a food processor and combine the stevia, cream cheese, and lemon zest.

Tips for Meal Prep:

1. Once combined, cover with foil or plastic wrap.
2. When it's breakfast time, toast the muffins.
3. Use a butter knife to spread the cheese mixture onto the toasted muffin halves. Add the berries and serve.

Dinner: Air-Fried Parmesan Chicken

Yields Provided: 4

Ingredients for Prep:

- Chicken breasts (2)
- Reduced-fat mozzarella cheese (6 tbsp.)
- Seasoned breadcrumbs (6 tbsp.)
- Olive oil/melted butter (1 tbsp.)
- Marinara sauce (.5 cup)
- Grated parmesan cheese (2 tbsp.)
- Cooking spray (as needed)

Method of Prep:

1. Warm the Air Fryer at 360° Fahrenheit for nine minutes. Chop the chicken in half to make four servings.
2. Combine the parmesan and breadcrumbs in one dish. In another dish, melt the butter. Lightly brush the butter over the chicken and dip in the mixture.
3. When the fryer is hot, just add two of the pieces in the basket and spray a layer of oil over the top of the chicken. Cook for six minutes and flip each piece. Chop each piece with 1 tablespoon of sauce and 1.5 tablespoons of the cheese.
4. Cook three more minutes and set aside to prepare the other two.
5. Repeat the process. Serve and enjoy or store for later.

Tips for Meal Prep:

1. Prepare the chicken and let it cool.
2. Store in a wrapper of foil.
3. Serve for one to two days and freeze at that time for the best results.

Snack: Baked Pumpkin Pie Egg Roll

Yields Provided: 4

Ingredients for Prep:

- Pumpkin puree (.75 cup)
- Greek yogurt (.25 cup)
- Pumpkin pie spice (1 tsp.)
- Brown sugar (2 tbsp.)
- Egg roll wrappers (4)
- Cooking spray
- Cinnamon
- Fat-free Cool-Whip

Method of Prep:

1. Set the oven temperature to 350° Fahrenheit.
2. Whisk the pie spice, brown sugar, pumpkin, and yogurt – mixing well.
3. Spread about ¼ cup of the pumpkin mixture in the middle of the wrapper.
4. Fold the bottom corner and run a line of water across the rest of the sides to act as glue. Prepare and close each of the rolls.
5. Arrange the rolls on a greased baking sheet, pizza stone, or parchment-lined pan.
6. Give the tops a spray of the cooking oil and bake until crispy (11 to 13 min.).

Tips for Meal Prep:

1. This super easy recipe is great anytime.
2. Let the cookies cool and store in an airtight cookie jar for later.

Week 2

Day 8

Breakfast: Overnight Oats with Bananas & Walnuts

Yields Provided: 1

Ingredients for Prep:

- Ground cinnamon (.25 tsp.)
- Low-fat or nonfat milk (.5 cup)
- Rolled oats (.5 cup)
- Mashed ripe banana (1)
- Chopped walnuts (2 tbsp.)
- Optional: Sweetener of choice as desired
- Also Needed: 1 mason jar

Method of Prep:
1. Fill the mason jar with the oats, cinnamon, banana, and walnuts.
2. Pour in the milk and place it in the fridge.

Tips for Meal Prep:
1. Let it sit overnight while you sleep or about 8 hours.
2. When serving, add more milk as desired.

Lunch: Heirloom Tomato & Cucumber Toast

Yields Provided: 1

Ingredients for Prep:

- Persian cucumber (1)
- Heirloom tomato (1 small)
- Olive oil (1 tsp.)
- Dried oregano (1 pinch)
- Black pepper and salt (to your liking)

For Serving:

- Low-fat whipped cream cheese (2 tsp.)
- Whole Grain Crispbread or another favorite (2 pieces)
- Balsamic glaze (1 tsp.)

Method of Prep:

1. Dice the cucumber and tomato.
2. Combine all of the fixings except for the cream cheese and glaze

Tips for Meal Prep:

1. Store the prepared mixture in a closed container until ready to serve.
2. Smear the cheese on the bread, and add the mixture (step 1).
3. Top it off with the balsamic glaze and serve.
4. Note: Increase the ingredient portions to suit your needs.

Dinner: Drumsticks with Apple Glaze

Yields Provided: 4

Ingredients for Prep:

- Apples (2)
- Molasses (.25 cup)
- Ground ginger (.5 tsp.)
- Apple butter (.25 cup)
- Salt (.5 tsp.)
- Freshly cracked black pepper (.25 tsp.)
- Lemon - juiced (half of 1)
- Chicken drumsticks (4 skin-on or skinless)

Method of Prep:

1. Core and slice the apple into 8 pieces. Sprinkle using the lemon juice.
2. Combine all of the components for the marinade. Add the drumsticks to the mixture. Marinate in the fridge for 15 minutes.
3. Warm the oven broiler. Prepare the broiler pan with foil. Arrange the drumsticks in the pan and broil for 12 to 15 minutes. Turn a couple of times and baste with the marinade.
4. Serve with sliced apple wedges.

Tips for Meal Prep:

1. Cool the chicken and add it into freezer bags for storage unless you will be eating it in the next day or two.
2. Wait to slice the apple until serving time.

Snack: Pumpkin Cookies

Yields Provided: 6

Ingredients for Prep:

- Whole wheat flour (2 cups)
- Baking soda (1 tsp.)
- Coconut sugar (1 cup)
- Old-fashioned oats (1 cup)
- Pumpkin pie spice (1 tsp.)
- Egg (1)
- Melted coconut oil (1 cup)
- Pumpkin puree (15 oz.)
- Roasted pumpkin seeds (.5 cup)
- Dried cherries (.5 cup)

Method of Prep:

1. Warm the oven to reach 350° Fahrenheit.
2. Prepare a baking tin with a sheet of aluminum foil.
3. Combine all of the fixings in a mixing container.
4. Mix well and shape into medium cookies.
5. Place each one on the baking tin.
6. Bake for approximately 25 minutes.

Tips for Meal Prep:

1. Move the pan to a cooling rack before storing or serving.
2. Enjoy whenever you want a healthy treat.

Day 9

Breakfast: Pineapple Oatmeal

Yields Provided: 4

Ingredients for Prep:

- Chopped walnuts (1 cup)
- Cubed pineapple (2 cups)
- Old-fashioned oats (2 cups)
- Nonfat milk (2 cups)
- Grated ginger (1 tbsp.)
- Eggs (2)
- Stevia or your favorite sweetener (2 tbsp.)
- Vanilla extract (2 tsp.)
- Also Needed: 4 ramekins

Method of Prep:

1. Set the oven temperature at 400° Fahrenheit.
2. Combine the oats with walnuts, pineapple, and ginger. Stir well and divide into the ramekins.
3. In a mixing container, combine the eggs with the milk, vanilla, and sweetener. Empty the egg mixture over the oats.
4. Arrange the ramekins in the oven and set a timer to bake for about 25 minutes.

Tips for Meal Prep:

1. Serve when ready or cool for storage.
2. Cover the ramekins with plastic wrap or foil and place in the refrigerator until it's mealtime.

3. Remove the wrap. Pop it into the microwave for 30 seconds with a splash of milk if needed. Serve.

Lunch: Baked Sweet Potatoes

Yields Provided: 3

Ingredients for Prep:
- Sliced onion (1)
- Sweet potatoes (3 diced)
- Freshly cracked black pepper & salt (.5 tsp. each)
- Cinnamon (5 tsp.)
- Olive oil (2 tbsp.)

Method of Prep:
1. Warm a skillet on the stovetop and pour in the oil. After it's heated, toss in the sliced onion and sauté for one to two minutes.
2. Set the oven temperature to 355° Fahrenheit.
3. Combine the potatoes with the onion and the remainder of the fixings.
4. Set a timer to bake for 30 to 35 minutes. Serve and enjoy!

Tips for Meal Prep:
1. Cool and store in the fridge for 2-3 days.
2. Warm in a 350° Fahrenheit oven.

Dinner: Lean Cheeseburgers

Yields Provided: 2

Ingredients for Prep:
- Whole-wheat hamburger buns - with seeds (4)
- 95% lean ground beef (1 lb.)
- Quick-cooking oats (2 tbsp.)
- Steak seasoning blend (.5 tsp.)
- Low-fat cheese - ex. cheddar or American (4 slices)
- Optional: Lettuce leaves & tomato slices

Method of Prep:
1. Split the burger buns in half.
2. Dump the oats into a plastic zipper-type baggie and securely seal. Squeeze out all of the excess air and use a rolling pin to crush the oats until they're a fine texture.
3. Mix the oats with the beef and steak seasoning. Shape into four - ½-inch patties.
4. Have the charcoal grill prepared until the coals are ash covered.
5. Place a lid on the grill to cook for 11 to 13 minutes, or you can use the medium heat setting on a gas grill and cook for 7 to 8 minutes. The thermometer inserted horizontally into the center should read 160° Fahrenheit.
6. Prepare the bun with lettuce and tomato if you're using it and top it off with a burger and a slice of cheese.
7. Close the sandwich and serve.

Tips for Meal Prep:
1. Follow all of the steps to step six.
2. Let the burgers cool thoroughly and wrap in plastic wrap. Place in freezer bags for storage.

Snack: Chocolate Pudding

Yields Provided: 4

Ingredients for Prep:
- Nonfat milk (2 cups)
- Salt (.125 tsp.)
- Cornstarch (3 tbsp.)
- Sugar (2 tbsp.)
- Cocoa powder (2 tbsp.)
- Vanilla (.5 tsp.)
- Chocolate chips (.33 cup)

Method of Prep:
1. Whisk the cornstarch, cocoa powder, salt, and sugar together. Stir in the milk.
2. Cook using the medium heat setting until it starts to boil and thicken.
3. Transfer to the countertop. Stir in the vanilla and chocolate chips.
4. Serve and chill until set using a layer of plastic wrap over the top of the bowl.

Tips for Meal Prep:
1. So easy, just prepare and scoop into individual dishes until you are ready to eat them.

Day 10

Breakfast: Cinnamon-Apple French Toast

Yields Provided: 4

Ingredients for Prep:

- Liquid egg whites (1.33 cups)
- 1% milk (1 cup)
- Eggs (4)
- Cinnamon (2 tsp.)
- Apples (2)
- Low-calorie bread (8 slices)
- *Also Needed*: 9x13 casserole dish

Method of Prep:

1. Peel and dice the apples. Grease the baking dish with cooking spray. Prepare the oven temperature to 350° Fahrenheit.
2. Use a microwavable dish to combine and cook the cinnamon and apples for three minutes.
3. Line the baking dish using bread slices and a layer of cooked apples.
4. Whisk the egg whites and milk. Pour over the bread.
5. Bake 45 minutes.

Tips for Meal Prep:

1. Let the mixture thoroughly cool.
2. Use a layer of aluminum foil or plastic wrap to cover the baking dish.
3. Refrigerate overnight.
4. When you're ready to eat, set the oven temperature at 350° Fahrenheit.
5. Discard the cover of the baking dish.
6. Bake until set and lightly browned.
7. Transfer the dish to the stovetop for 10 minutes.
8. Serve with your favorite toppings.

Lunch: Leftover Turkey Noodle Soup

Yields Provided: 4

Ingredients for Prep:
- Turkey stock – low-sodium canned/homemade (6 cups)
- Bay leaf (1)
- Garlic cloves (2)
- Carrot (1 cup)
- Onion (.75 cup)
- Celery (.75 cup)
- Salt (as desired)
- Freshly cracked black pepper
- Fresh parsley (.25 cup)
- No-yolk egg noodles (3 oz.)
- Leftover shredded turkey (8 oz. - 2 cups)

Method of Prep:
1. Fill a large soup pot with the turkey stock.
2. Dice the carrot, garlic, onion, and celery. Mince the garlic.
3. Add the bay leaf, celery, onion, carrots, salt, and black pepper to your liking. Simmer until the vegetables are softened (10-15 min.).
4. Chop and toss in the parsley, shredded turkey, and noodles Simmer for about five minutes. Discard the bay leaf and serve.

1. Chill the soup and pour it into four individual containers.
2. Serve as needed over the next day or two.

Dinner: Honey Grilled Chicken

Yields Provided: 2

Ingredients for Prep:

- Margarine (2 tbsp.)
- Minced garlic (1 clove)
- Chicken breast (4 halves)
- Honey (.33 cup)
- Lemon (1 juiced)

Method of Prep:
1. Prepare the grill using the medium heat setting.
2. Use the medium heat setting on the stovetop to melt the margarine. Toss in the minced garlic and simmer slowly for two minutes. Whisk the juice and honey and spread half over the breasts.
3. Spritz the grill with oil. Arrange the chicken on the grate. Cook for 5-8 minutes per side. Baste with the rest of the sauce at the end of the cooking cycle.
4. The chicken will be firm with clear juices when poked with a fork.

Tips for Meal Prep:

1. Cool the chicken and place into individual or containers of veggies for a complete meal option.

Snack: Cranberry & Apple Dessert Risotto

Yields Provided: 4

Ingredients for Prep:
- Fat-free milk (3.5 cups)
- Apple (1)
- Dried cranberries (.5 cup)
- Arborio rice (.5 cup)
- Butter (1 tbsp.)
- Apple cider (1.5 cups)
- Salt (1 dash)
- Light brown sugar (2 tbsp.)

Method of Prep:
1. Measure and add the dried cranberries into a bowl of water. Wait for them to plump.
2. Combine the salt, cinnamon, and milk in a saucepan. Once it is hot, transfer the pan to the countertop to steep.
3. Melt the butter in another pan. Add the sliced/diced apple. Stir often until most of the juices are absorbed. Stir in the sugar/milk mixture.
4. Cook until the rice has a creamy texture. Discard the cinnamon stick and drain the cranberries.
5. Stir in the risotto. Serve warm.

Tips for Meal Prep:
1. Cool and scoop into four containers for a quick on the go snack

Day 11

Breakfast: Oatmeal & Blueberry Muffins

Yields Provided: 12

Ingredients for Prep:
- Unsweetened almond milk (1 cup)
- Canola oil (1 tbsp.)
- Oats (1.5 cups)
- Baking soda (.5 tsp.)
- Salt (.5 tsp.)
- Baking powder (1 tsp.)
- All-purpose flour (.66 cup)

Method of Prep:
1. Use a blender to pulse the oats and soak in the milk for a minimum of 30 minutes.
2. Set the oven temperature to 400° Fahrenheit.
3. Prepare the muffin tins.
4. Whisk the baking soda, salt, baking powder, canola oil, vanilla extract, honey, and applesauce. Mix well.
5. Fold in the brown sugar, soaked oats, and flour. Mix and divide into the prepared tins.
6. Bake about 24 minutes until the tops are nicely browned.

Tips for Meal Prep:
1. Take the muffin tin out of the oven.
2. Set out on the countertop.
3. Once cooled, store them in a plastic bag, seal at room temperature for up to three days.

Lunch: Ravioli Lasagna

Yields Provided: 6-8

Ingredients for Prep:
- Frozen ravioli (1 lb.)
- Pasta sauce (24 oz.)
- Frozen chopped spinach (8 oz. pkg.)
- Fat-free ricotta (15 oz.)
- Minced garlic (1 tsp.)
- Mozzarella (2 cups - shredded)
- Also Needed: 9x13 pan

Method of Prep:
1. Break up the frozen spinach into a small bowl and mix in the garlic and ricotta.
2. Pour a thin layer of sauce over the bottom part of the pan.
3. Lay down the first layer of ravioli, top with half the spinach mixture, 1/3 of the red sauce, then ½ cup of mozzarella. Repeat this layer again.
4. Top with remaining ravioli, red sauce, and mozzarella.

Tips for Meal Prep:
1. Eat it Now or Prep to Freeze: Set the oven at 375° Fahrenheit Place a layer of foil over the pan and bake for 30 minutes Discard the layer of foil and continue baking an additional ten minutes until golden and bubbly. Serve.
2. Cool thoroughly and cover with plastic wrap, pressing down to remove as much air as possible, then cover with foil. Label with the date and contents before freezing.
3. Baking from Frozen: Remove the plastic and foil, and cover again with foil. Warm the oven to 375° Fahrenheit. Set a timer and bake for one hour. Remove the foil and bake for ten minutes more minutes until golden, bubbly and all the pasta is cooked through.

Dinner: Ground Pork Loaf

Yields Provided: 4

Ingredients for Prep:
- Red onions (1 small)
- Garlic (2 cloves)
- Olive oil (1 tbsp.)
- Lemon - juiced and zested (1)
- Cherry tomatoes (1-pint)
- Black pepper (as desired)
- Basil (1 tbsp.)
- Low-sodium tomato paste (2 tbsp.)
- Low-sodium vegetable stock (.5 cup)

Method of Prep:
1. Pour the water into a skillet and let it heat up.
2. Mince the garlic. Chop the onions, tomatoes, and basil. When hot, toss in the onion and garlic. Cook slowly for about five minutes.
3. Stir in the tomatoes, stock, lemon juice and zest, tomato paste, black pepper, and the pork. Stir well and cook for 15 minutes.
4. Garnish with the basil and serve when ready.

Tips for Meal Prep:
1. Allow the meat to totally cool.
2. Portion into the chosen freezer container.
3. Defrost and use it as needed.

Snack: Applesauce

Yields Provided: 3-4

Ingredients for Prep:
- Granny Smith apples (1 lb.)
- Water (1 cup)
- Lemon juice (1 tbsp.)
- Sugar (.5 cup)

Method of Prep:
1. Peel, core, and chop the apples.
2. Fill a large pot of water using just enough to cover the apples.
3. Simmer the apples until softened or for about 20 minutes. Add them to a blender or food processor.
4. Pour in the lemon juice and sugar. Pulse until well combined.
5. Add the mixture back into the pot and simmer 4-5 additional minutes.

Tips for Meal Prep:
1. Cool thoroughly and scoop into individual bowls for a quick and healthy on-the-go snack.

Day 12

Breakfast: Cantaloupe Blueberry Breakfast Bowl

Yields Provided: 2

Ingredients for Prep:

- Whole cantaloupe (1)
- Blueberries (1 cup)
- Cottage cheese (1.5 cups)
- Chopped pecans (.25 cup)
- Hemp seeds (2 tbsp.)

Method of Prep:

1. Wash and pat dry the cantaloupe; slice in half.
2. Chop the pecans and add with the hemp seeds in a small container.
3. Store the cantaloupe with a layer of plastic wrap.

Tips for Meal Prep:

1. Time to Serve: Scoop a ¾ cup serving of the cottage cheese into each half.
2. Garnish both portions with the pecans/seed mix and blueberries.
3. Serve and enjoy it immediately.

Lunch: Pizza Logs

Yields Provided: 8

Ingredients for Prep:
- Egg roll wrappers (8)
- Pizza sauce - your healthy option (8 tsp.)
- Italian seasoning (1 tsp.)
- Light mozzarella string cheese sticks (4 - cut into halves)
- Turkey-pepperoni slices (24)

Method of Prep:
1. Warm the oven to reach 425° Fahrenheit.
2. Lightly mist a large baking tray using a spritz of cooking oil spray and set aside.
3. Prepare a dish of water as a fingertip dish.
4. Arrange each egg roll wrapper on a flat surface with the corner facing toward you.
5. Spread 1 tsp. of sauce across the center of the wrapper, leaving 0.5-inch on each side.
6. Sprinkle Italian seasoning, a row of 3 pepperoni slices, and half of a cheese stick.
7. Fold the bottom corner over the fixings and roll. Fold the side corners in and tuck them as you give the filled section another roll.
8. Dampen the edges of the remaining corner of the wrapper. Finish rolling the filled log to close and place on the baking tray.
9. Arrange the wrapped log on the baking sheet. Continue with the remainder of the fixings.
10. Once they're all wrapped and ready on the baking tray, lightly spritz the tops using a portion of cooking oil spray.
11. Bake for 10 to 14 minutes. Flip them over about halfway through the cooking process.

Tips for Meal Prep:
1. Cool and keep in the refrigerator for a few days for the most flavorful results (if they last that long).

Dinner: Lemon Chicken

Yields Provided: 2

Ingredients for Prep:

- Lemon (1)
- Breasts of chicken (2)
- Oregano (1 pinch)
- Olive oil (1 tbsp.)
- Salt & Pepper (to your liking)

Method of Prep:

1. Discard the bones and skin from the chicken. Squeeze juice from the lemons over the chicken.
2. Sprinkle using pepper and salt.
3. Use medium heat to warm up the oil in a skillet on the stovetop. Cook the chicken. As it is cooking, sprinkle with oregano and additional pepper or salt as desired.
4. Poke it with a fork. It's done when the juices in the center of the chicken run clear.

Tips for Meal Prep:

1. Portion into freezer bags and defrost as a quick base for dinner.

Snack: Lemony Banana Mix

Yields Provided: 4

Ingredients for Prep:
- Strawberries (5)
- Banana (4)
- Lemons (2)
- Coconut sugar (4 tbsp.)

Method of Prep:
1. Juice the lemons and slice the strawberries into halves. Peel and chop the bananas.
2. In a mixing bowl, combine all of the fixings.
3. Toss well and serve cold.

Tips for Meal Prep:
1. Serve over the next couple of days.
2. Store in a covered container or individual dishes.

Day 13

Breakfast: Cherries & Oats

Yields Provided: 6

Ingredients for Prep:

- Water (6 cups)
- Almond milk (1 cup)
- Cinnamon (1 tsp.)
- Old-fashioned oats (2 cups)
- Vanilla extract (1 tsp.)
- Cherries (2 cups)

Method of Prep:

1. Remove the pits and slice the cherries.
2. Combine all of the fixings in a small pot.
3. Bring the pot to a boil using the medium-high heat setting.
4. Cook the mixture for 15 minutes and divide it into serving containers or in one dish.

Tips for Meal Prep:

1. Wait for the oatmeal cool to touch (about one hour).
2. Cover tightly and place in the fridge.
3. If using individual jars for oatmeal storage, microwave for two to three minutes until hot.

Lunch: Turkey & Pear Pita Melt

Yields Provided: 1

Ingredients for Prep:
- Sliced pear (1)
- Deli turkey – low-sodium (3.5 oz.)
- Mixed greens (1 cup)
- Shredded cheddar cheese (1 tbsp.)
- Large whole wheat pita (half of 1)

Method of Prep:
1. Slice the pear and rinse the greens.
2. Stuff the pita with the turkey, cheese, and pears.
3. Place in a toaster oven if you have one, or use the main oven.
4. When warm, add the greens to the hot pita and enjoy the remainder of the pear slices on the side of the dish.

Tips for Meal Prep:
1. Prepare the pita, but don't toast it until it is time to eat.
2. Store in the fridge until mealtime.

Dinner: Pork Chops & Apples

Yields Provided: 4

Ingredients for Prep:

- Low-sodium chicken stock (1.5 cups)
- Pork chops (4)
- Black pepper (as desired)
- Yellow chopped onion (1)
- Minced garlic cloves (2)
- Chopped thyme (1 tbsp.)
- Cored & sliced apples (3)
- Olive oil (1 tbsp.)

Method of Prep:

1. Heat the oven until it reaches 350° Fahrenheit.
2. Pour the oil into a pan. Set the temperature on medium-high.
3. When hot, add the pork chops and sprinkle with the pepper.
4. Cook for five minutes per side.
5. Add the garlic, onion, lime, apples, and the stock.
6. Toss well and add the mixture to a baking dish. Set a timer and bake for 50 minutes.
7. Serve when ready.

Tips for Meal Prep:

1. Prepare the dish until ready. Set aside to thoroughly cool.
2. Store in a sectional container or individual container and pop into the freezer.

Snack: Delicious Apple Pie

Yields Provided: 8

Ingredients for Prep:
For the Crust:
- Dry rolled oats (1 cup)
- Ground almonds (.25 cup)
- Whole wheat pastry flour (.25 cup)
- Packed brown sugar (2 tbsp.)
- Water (1 tbsp.)
- Canola oil (3 tbsp.)

For the Filling:
- Frozen apple juice concentrate (.33 cup)
- Tart apples (6 cups or 4 large)
- Cinnamon (1 tsp.)
- Quick-cooking tapioca (2 tbsp.)

Method of Prep:
1. Heat the oven to reach 425° Fahrenheit.
2. Prepare the Pie Crust: Combine the dry fixings in one mixing bowl and the dry in another. Combine the two until a dough is formed. Blend together until the dough sticks together. You may need more or less water.
3. Press the dough into a nine-inch pie plate. Set aside.
4. Prepare the Filling: Peel and slice the apples. Mix all of the fixings. Let it stand for about 15 minutes. Stir and place into the pie crust.
5. Bake for 15 minutes at 425° Fahrenheit, reducing the heat for the last 40 minutes at 350° Fahrenheit.

Tips for Meal Prep:
1. You have about two days to enjoy your pies unchilled at room temperature.
2. If the pie has been sliced, place them into a container and loosely cover loosely using plastic wrap. The pie will keep for another two to three days in the fridge.

Day 14

Breakfast: Tropical Breakfast Pie

Yields Provided: 4

Ingredients for Prep:

- Granulated sugar (.5 tsp.)
- Unsweetened shredded coconut (2 tbsp.)
- Refrigerated biscuit dough (7.5 oz.)
- Fresh pineapple (1 cup)
- *Also Needed*: 8-inch-square casserole dish

Method of Prep:

1. Warm up the oven in advance to 350° Fahrenheit.
2. Lightly coat the casserole dish with a splash of cooking spray. Break apart the dough into ten portions and slice into quarters.
3. Load a zipper-type bag with the sugar and coconut. Shake and add the dough bits. Shake gently, but thoroughly to coat.
4. Place the biscuits into the dish and garnish with the diced pineapple.
5. Bake for 25 minutes.

Tips for Meal Prep:

1. Transfer to the counter to cool before placing it in the refrigerator.
2. Serve yourself whenever you need a quick and healthy breakfast dish.

Lunch: Baked Macaroni with Red Sauce

Yields Provided: 6

Ingredients for Prep:
- Diced onion (.5 cup)
- Whole-wheat elbow macaroni (7 oz.)
- Spaghetti sauce - reduced-sodium or homemade (15 oz.)
- Extra-lean beef (.5 lb.)
- Parmesan cheese (6 tbsp.)

Method of Prep:
1. Set the oven to 350° Fahrenheit. Spritz a casserole baking dish with cooking oil spray.
2. Sauté the onions and beef in a frying pan until the onion is fragrant. Drain the grease out of the pan.
3. Fill a pot with water and prepare the pasta until tender or about 10 to 12 minutes. Empty the mixture into a mesh colander to drain.
4. Combine the pasta with the meat and add the sauce. Stir and scoop into the prepared dish. Bake for 25 to 35 minutes.
5. Serve and enjoy each serving with 1 tablespoon of the cheese.

Tips for Meal Prep:
1. Properly stored in closed containers, homemade pasta, and the sauce will last for 2 to 3 days in the fridge.
2. Freeze it in heavy-duty freezer bags.

Dinner: BARBECUE Ranch Chicken Bites

Yields Provided: 4-6

Ingredients for Prep:

- Ranch dressing (.66 cup)
- BARBECUE sauce (.33 cup)
- Chicken breasts (2 lb.)
- Optional: Finely chopped fresh chives (1 tbsp.)
- Skewers (10 - 9 to 12-inch)

Method of Prep:

1. If you are using wooden skewers, soak in water for at least 15 minutes. Prepare a rimmed baking sheet using a sheet of foil and spritz with a misting of cooking spray.
2. Pour the ranch dressing and BARBECUE sauce in a large mixing bowl. Stir to combine. Transfer half to a small serving bowl, cover, and refrigerate. Remove the skin and bones from the chicken, cut it into 1-inch chunks, and add it to the remaining sauce. Toss to combine.
3. Marinate for about half an hour on the countertop or cover and refrigerate for up to 24 hours. (The ideal time is about 2 hours. At 24 hours, the chicken is very tender but starts to break down slightly.)
4. When ready to cook, arrange a rack 4 to 5 inches from the heating element and warm the oven to broil.
5. Thread the chicken onto the skewers, 6 to 7 pieces per skewer. Place the skewers (not touching) on the baking sheet. Broil until charred in spots and cooked through, or about 8 minutes. Top with chives, if using, and serve with the reserved sauce for dipping.

Tips for Meal Prep:

1. After the chicken is prepared, either store in the fridge for 3-4 days or put into individual freezer bags until needed.

Snack: Wacky Chocolate Cake

Yields Provided: 6

Ingredients for Prep:
- Whole wheat pastry flour (3 cups)
- Unsweetened cocoa powder (3 tbsp.)
- Sugar (1 cup)
- Salt (.5 tsp)
- Baking soda (2.25 tsp.)
- Vinegar (2 tbsp.)
- Vanilla (1 tbsp.)
- Hot water (2 cups)
- Canola oil (.5 cup)

Method of Prep:
1. Warm up the oven to reach 350° Fahrenheit.
2. Likely spritz a baking dish with cooking oil spray.
3. Whisk the baking soda, salt, sugar, and cocoa powder.
4. Stir in the oil, vinegar, and vanilla.
5. Slowly pour in the water as you whisk the mixture for about 2 minutes.
6. Dump the batter into the baking dish and set a timer to bake for 30 minutes.
7. When cool, slice into 18 squares and serve.

Tips for Meal Prep:
1. Cool the cake and store it in a closed container.
2. It should be good for three days.

Chapter 6: Delicious Snacks Dips & Spreads

Black Bean Brownies – Vegan

Yields Provided: 12

Ingredients for Prep:
- Black beans (1.5 cups)
- Unsweetened applesauce (.25 cup)
- Blackstrap molasses (.25 cup)
- All-purpose flour (.25 cup)
- Unsweetened cocoa powder (.33 cup)
- Salt (.5 tsp.)
- Baking powder (.5 tsp.)
- *Also Needed*:
- 8x8 casserole dish
- Cooking spray
- Food processor or blender

Method of Prep:

1. Set the oven in advance to 375° Fahrenheit. Spray the dish with the spray.
2. Drain and rinse the beans and add them to the blender. Pulse until fairly smooth. Dump into a container with the molasses and applesauce. Stir.
3. Sift in the salt, flour, cocoa powder, and baking powder. Mix well.
4. Pour into the prepared dish and bake 35 minutes.
5. Perform the toothpick test for doneness. If it's clean when inserted into the center of the brownies, it's done.

Tips for Meal Prep:

1. Let the brownies cool after they are done.
2. Make a double batch; store one and freeze one!

Breakfast Cookies

Yields Provided: 12 cookies

Ingredients for Prep:
- Rolled oats (2 cups)
- Large bananas (2 mashed)
- Chocolate chips (.75 cup)

Method of Prep:
1. Warm the oven to 350° Fahrenheit.
2. Stir the oats and bananas until they are thoroughly combined.
3. Stir in chocolate chips.
4. Roll the cookies into 2-inch balls, and then flatten to make the cookie shape.
5. Bake on a parchment paper-lined cookie sheet for 12 minutes.

Tips for Meal Prep:
1. Cool thoroughly and store in closed containers until ready to eat.

Chocolate Biscotti

Yields Provided: 15

Ingredients for Prep:
- Large egg (1)
- Monk fruit sweetener or erythritol (.25 cup)
- Stevia concentrated powder (.25 tsp.)
- Softened butter (.25 cup)
- Vanilla extract (.5 tsp.)
- Almond flour (1.75 cups)
- Xanthan gum (.25 tsp.)
- Unsweetened cocoa (.5 cup)
- Baking soda (.5 tsp.)
- Sea salt (.25 tsp.)
- Cinnamon (1 tsp.)
- *Optional:* Sugar-free chocolate chips
- *Optional:* Chopped nuts

Method of Prep:
1. Set the oven to reach 325° Fahrenheit.
2. Mix the butter with the egg, stevia, granular sweetener, and vanilla.
3. In another container, sift or whisk all the dry fixings and mix until well incorporated.
4. Combine the wet and dry fixings, stirring as you go. Chocolate chips or nuts can be mixed in at this time.
5. Prepare the ball of dough. Arrange the dough ball on a layer of parchment baking paper, silicone baking mat or cookie sheet. Shape the dough into a long flat log.
6. Bake for approximately 18 to 20 minutes. Transfer from the oven and lower the heat setting to 275° Fahrenheit. Cool for about 10 minutes. Slice into thin strips about .5-inch wide.

Orange Cream Cheese Cookies & Nuts

Yields Provided: 18

Ingredients for Prep:
- Softened butter (.75 cup)
- Eggs (3)
- Coconut flour (.5 cup)
- Baking powder (1.5 tsp.)
- Monk fruit sweetener (.75 cup)
- Baking soda (.25 tsp.)
- Sugar-free dried cranberries (.25 cup)
- Macadamia nuts chopped (.5 cup)
- Dried grated orange zest (1.5 tsp.)

Method of Prep:
1. In a mixing container, beat the sweetener with the eggs and butter until well combined.
2. Whisk or sift the coconut flour, baking powder, and soda. Beat on the low setting or with a spoon until fully mixed.
3. Fold in the berries, orange zest, and nuts.
4. Shape into rounds and arrange on the cookie sheet.
5. Arrange the cookies a minimum of one inch apart for baking on a parchment-lined cookie sheet. Press each mound down slightly to flatten.
6. Bake at 350° Fahrenheit until edges have started to brown or for eight to ten minutes.

Tips for Meal Prep:
1. Cool on a cooling rack.
2. Enjoy right out of the fridge for a week, or they can be frozen for longer storage.

Peanut Butter Bites

Yields Provided: 2 bites

Ingredients for Prep:
- Rolled oats (1.5 cups)
- Natural peanut butter - for nut-free use sunflower seed butter (.5 cup)
- Honey or maple syrup (3 tbsp.)

Method of Prep:
1. Add the oats to a food processor or blender. Blend until oats reach a flour consistency.
2. Next, add the peanut butter and honey or maple syrup. Process until the fixings are well combined and come together to form a dough ball. You may need to scrape the sides once or twice.
3. Roll into round bites – about a scant tablespoon per bite. If the dough isn't holding together, add one to two tablespoons more of the peanut butter.
4. If the dough starts to stick to your hands, oil them with coconut oil or cooking spray.

Tips for Meal Prep:
1. Store the *Peanut Butter Bites* in an airtight container in the fridge for up to 2 weeks.

Tag-along Cookies Copycat Girl Scout™ Cookies

Yields Provided: 12

Ingredients for Prep:
- Vanilla wafer cookies (12)
- Chocolate chips (.5 cup)
- Creamy peanut butter (3 tbsp.)
- Coconut oil (.25 tsp.)

Method of Prep:
1. Spread the peanut butter on the wafers and place them on a parchment paper-lined cookie tin.
2. Place the chocolate chips in the microwave at 15-second intervals until melted. Add a splash of coconut oil to make the chips smoother.
3. Dip the wafers into the chocolate to cover and place it on the paper-lined pan.

Tips for Meal Prep:
1. Cool thoroughly and place it in the fridge to set.
2. Cover and eat as desired.

3 Ingredient Reese's Fudge

Yields Provided: 24

Ingredients for Prep:
- Vanilla frosting - not fluffy (1 container)
- Mini Reese's Pieces (10 oz. bag)
- Peanut butter cups (10 oz.)

Method of Prep:
1. Discard the foil wrapper from the frosting and microwave the container for 30 seconds.
2. Add the peanut butter chips in another container and microwave for one minute.
3. Stir it all together and toss in about ¾ of the bag into the mixture.
4. Grease the baking tin and add the fudge.

Tips for Meal Prep:
1. Before slicing into squares for storage, be sure it is thoroughly cooled (about 30 minutes.

Movie Night Popcorn Galore

These are a sure way to enjoy movies on a budget! Just choose the desired flavors.

Prepare the popcorn in advance and combine the chosen topping from these:

Birthday Cake Popcorn

Yields Provided: 4

Ingredients for Prep:
- Melted white chocolate chips (1 cup)
- Biscoff spread (1 tbsp.)
- Betty Crocker ™ candy sprinkles (2 tbsp.)
- Popcorn (8 cups)

Method of Prep:
1. Melt the chocolate chips and mix in the Bischoff spread.
2. Drizzle over the prepared popcorn and top with the sprinkles.
3. Cool before serving.

Caramel Apple Popcorn

Yields Provided: 10

Ingredients for Prep:
- Popped popcorn (12 cups)
- Brown sugar (1 cup)
- Light corn syrup (.25 cup)
- Salt (.5 tsp.)
- Baking soda (.5 tsp.)
- Vanilla (1 tsp.)
- Cinnamon chips (1 cup)
- Toffee bit (1 cup)
- Whole pecans (1 cup)
- Dried apple chips (1 cup)
- Butter (1 tbsp.)

Method of Prep:
1. Place the brown sugar, light corn syrup, salt, and butter in a microwave-safe bowl.
2. Microwave for about 1 minute, just until the butter is melted, then stir together until well mixed.
3. Return to the microwave and cook for 2 minutes, stir, then cook for an additional 2 minutes.
4. Add the baking soda and vanilla to the caramel. Stir until well mixed.
5. Place your popped popcorn in a large bowl and drizzle the caramel over the popcorn.
6. Sprinkle the cinnamon chips, toffee bits, pecans, and dried apple chips over the popcorn. Toss lightly. Allow cooling before serving.

Chocolate Coffee Peanut Butter Pretzel Popcorn

Yields Provided: 4

Ingredients for Prep:

- Popcorn (8 cups)
- Instant coffee grounds (.5 tbsp.)
- Crushed peanut butter pretzels (.5 cup)
- Chocolate bars - melted (2 bars/4 oz.) or Dark chocolate chips (1.5 cups)

Method of Prep:
1. Melt the chocolate and stir in the grounds of coffee.
2. Drizzle and toss over the popcorn with the pretzels.
3. Let the chocolate harden (room temp) before serving.

Cool Ranch Popcorn

Yields Provided: 4

Ingredients for Prep:
- Melted butter (.25 cup)
- White cheddar mac & cheese powder (2 tbsp.)
- Dry ranch dressing mix (2 tbsp.)
- Smoked paprika (.5 tsp.)
- Popcorn (8 cups)

Method of Prep:
1. Drizzle the prepared butter over the popcorn.
2. Whisk and sprinkle with the spice combo (paprika, cheddar & ranch powder).
3. Toss gently and serve.

Sriracha Popcorn

Yields Provided: 4

Ingredients for Prep:
- Melted butter (.25 cup)
- Sriracha (2 tbsp.)
- Garlic (1 clove)
- Popcorn (8 cups)

Method of Prep:
1. Mince the garlic and melt the butter.
2. Whisk the garlic, Sriracha, and butter to pour over the popcorn.
3. Enjoy immediately.

Dips & Spreads

Baked Potato Dip

Yields Provided: 8

Ingredients for Prep:
- Crispy crumbled turkey bacon (2 strips)
- Chives (1 tbsp.)
- Shredded 2% cheddar sharp cheese (.33 cup)
- Onion powder (.125 tsp.)
- Black pepper (.125 tsp.)
- Garlic powder (.125 tsp.)
- Salt (.125 tsp.)
- Fat-free sour cream (1 cup)

Method of Prep:
1. Brown the bacon until it's crispy and combine with the rest of the fixings.
2. Cool in the refrigerator for a minimum of one hour.

Tips for Meal Prep:
1. Be sure to let the dip cool completely.
2. Store in the refrigerator.
3. Serve with a tray of tasty veggies.

Italian Basil Pesto – Vegan

Yields Provided: 8 Servings - 2 tbsp. each

Ingredients for Prep:

- Tightly packed basil leaves (1 cup)
- Garlic cloves (2 large)
- Lemon juice (1 tbsp.)
- Lemon zest (1 tsp.)
- Toasted pine nuts (2 tbsp.)
- Olive oil (1 tbsp.)
- Water (.25 cup)
- Sea salt and freshly cracked pepper (to your liking)
- *Also Needed*: Food processor

Method of Prep:

1. Toss the pine nuts, lemon juice and zest, basil, and garlic into the processor. Blend until smooth, yet fairly chunky.
2. Pour in the oil and water to process until almost smooth.
3. Remove and place in a serving dish with a sprinkle of salt and pepper to your liking.
4. Stir and let the flavors blend for about ½ hour before serving.

Tips for Meal Prep:

1. Prepare the pesto as described.
2. Pour the mixture into a mason jar and serve any time.

Jalapeno - Bacon & Corn-Cheese Dip

Yields Provided: 3

Ingredients for Prep:
- Parmesan cheese (.25 cup)
- Shredded cheddar cheese (2 cups)
- Softened cream cheese (8 oz.)
- Drained corn (2 cans - 15 oz. each or as desired)
- Diced jalapenos (.25 cup)
- Bacon strips (8 cooked and crumbled)

Method of Prep:
1. Set the oven temperature to 400° Fahrenheit.
2. Prepare a cast iron skillet with a portion of cooking spray.
3. Combine all of the fixings, mixing well, and add to the pan.
4. Bake 20 minutes and serve.

Tips for Meal Prep:
1. Prepare the mixture for the dip and let it cool.
2. Store in the fridge in an airtight dish.
3. Serve as a delicious snack.

Pea Guacamole with Tortilla Chips

Yields Provided: 1

Ingredients for Prep:

- Avocado (¼ of 1 medium)
- Frozen green peas (.25 cup - thawed)
- Fresh lime juice (2 tsp.)
- Chopped uncooked red onion (2 tsp.)
- Cilantro (1 tbsp. - chopped)
- Table salt (.125 tsp.)
- Fresh tomatoes (1 tbsp. - chopped)
- Chips (7)

Method of Prep:

1. Use a blender or mini food processor to puree the lime juice with the peas and avocado.
2. Once it's smooth, stir in the onion, salt, and cilantro.

Tips for Meal Prep:

1. Store in the fridge until needed.
2. Serve with a portion of cilantro, onion, and tomato. Serve with a side of chips.

Spiced Smoky Red Pepper Dip

Yields Provided: 8 Servings /.25 cup each

Ingredients for Prep:
- Roasted red peppers - packed in water (32 oz.)
- Walnut oil (2.5 tsp.)
- Smoked variety paprika (1.25 tsp.)
- Finely chopped garlic (1 medium clove)
- Ground cumin (.5 tsp.)
- Table salt (.25 tsp.)
- Fresh oregano or chopped parsley (1 tbsp.)

Method of Prep:
1. Rinse and drain the peppers.
2. Puree all of the fixings, except for the oregano or parsley, in a blender or food processor.

Tips for Meal Prep:
1. Store in a glass container until time to serve.
2. Garnish with fresh herbs and serve.

Conclusion

I hope you have enjoyed your new collection of recipes in the *Meal Prep Cookbook for Beginners*. I hope it was informative and provided you with all of the tools you need to achieve your goals, whatever they may be.

The next step is to prepare a list of the cooking equipment and ingredients you will need to get started using your new techniques for meal prep. The suggestions provided were tested by the pros and are some of the easiest ones you will discover if you search the Internet. The guesswork is removed with the detailed instructions.

Finally, if you found this book useful in any way, a review on Amazon is always appreciated!

Index of Recipes

Breakfast: Omelet Waffles
Lunch: Chicken-Apple-Spinach Salad
Dinner: Apricot BARBECUE Chicken
Snack: Veggie Egg Cups

Day 7:
Breakfast: Banana Oat Pancakes
Lunch: Ham Salad
Dinner: Baked Chicken Fajita
Snack: Mini Crustless Quiche

Week 2:

Day 8:
Breakfast: Veggie Egg Scramble
Lunch: Asparagus Soup
Dinner: Asian Glazed Chicken
Snack: Veggie Snack Pack

Day 9:
Breakfast: Spinach - Feta & Egg Breakfast Quesadillas
Lunch: Salmon Vegetable Frittata
Dinner: Thai Peanut Chicken
Snack: Beef & Cheddar Roll-Ups

Day 10:
Breakfast: Breakfast Bowls
Lunch: Chili Con Carne
Dinner: Cajun Chicken
Snack: Fruit Snack Pack

Day 11:
Breakfast: Carrot Muffins
Lunch: Classic Stuffed Peppers
Dinner: Cilantro Lime Chicken
Snack: Avocado Hummus Snack Jars

Day 12:

Breakfast: Buckwheat Pancakes
Lunch: One-Tray Caprese Pasta
Dinner: Shrimp Taco Bowls
Snack: Vanilla Cashew Butter Cups
Day 13:
Breakfast: Corn & Apple Muffins
Lunch: Smoked Sausage & Orzo
Dinner: Chicken & Broccoli
Snack: Protein Sack Pack

Day 14:
Breakfast: Veggies & Eggs
Lunch: Starbucks™ Protein Bistro Box
Dinner: Sweet & Sour Meatballs
Snack: Ham – Swiss & Spinach Roll-Ups

Chapter 4: Keto Diet

Week 1:
Day 1:

Breakfast: Almost McGriddle Casserole
Lunch: Caesar Salmon Salad
Dinner: Chipotle Roast
Snack: Peanut Butter Protein Bars

Day 2:
Breakfast: Jalapeno Cheddar Waffles
Lunch: Chicken 'Zoodle' Soup
Dinner: Chicken Nuggets
Snack: Blueberry Cream Cheese Fat Bombs

Day 3:
Breakfast: Baked Green Eggs
Lunch: Mushroom & Cauliflower Risotto
Dinner: Chili Lime Cod
Snack: Coffee Fat Bombs

Day 4:
Breakfast: Vegan Gingerbread Muffins
Lunch: Spicy Beef Wraps
Dinner: Asparagus & Chicken
Snack: Mocha Cheesecake Bars

Day 5:
Breakfast: Egg Loaf
Lunch: BARBECUE Pork Loin
Dinner: Short Ribs
Snack: Delicious No-Bake Coconut Cookies

Day 6:
Breakfast: Spinach Quiche
Lunch: BLT Salad in a Jar
Dinner: Buffalo Chicken Burgers

Snack: Spice Cakes

Day 7:
Breakfast: Morning Hot Pockets
Lunch: Greek Salad
Dinner: Buffalo Sloppy Joes
Snack: Brownie Muffins

Week 2:

Day 8:

Breakfast: Avocado Eggs
Lunch: Tuna Salad
Dinner: Bacon & Shrimp Risotto
Snack: Pumpkin Pie Cupcakes

Day 9:
Breakfast: Tomato & Cheese Frittata
Lunch: Beef & Pepperoni Pizza
Dinner: Chicken & Green Beans
Snack: Amaretti Cookies

Day 10:
Breakfast: Blueberry Pancake Bites
Lunch: Buffalo Chicken Burgers
Dinner: Roasted Leg of Lamb

Day 11:
Breakfast: Blueberry Essence
Lunch: Italian Tomato Salad
Dinner: Bacon Cheeseburger
Snack: Strawberry Cream Cheese Bites

Day 12:
Breakfast: Pancakes & Nuts
Lunch: Pulled Pork for Sandwiches

Dinner: Shrimp Alfredo
Snack: Coconut Macaroons

Day 13:
Breakfast: Cinnamon Smoothie
Lunch: Pita Pizza
Dinner: Roasted Chicken & Tomatoes
Snack: Pecan Turtle Truffles

Day 14:
Breakfast: Bacon Cheese & Egg Cups
Lunch: Caprese Salad
Dinner: Enchilada Skillet Dinner

Chapter 5: Meal Prep Recipes for Kids

Week 1:

Day 1:
Breakfast: Apple Banana Muffins
Lunch: Cranberry Tuna Salad
Dinner: Hawaiian Chicken Kebabs
Snack: Apple Pie Cookies

Day 2:
Breakfast: Mango Smoothie Base & Oats
Lunch: Buffalo Chicken Tenders
Dinner: Chili & Mac 'n' Cheese
Snack: Pumpkin Cupcakes

Day 3:
Breakfast: Banana Almond Pancakes
Lunch: Colored Iceberg Salad
Dinner: Delicious Meatloaf
Snack: Whole Grain Banana Bread

Day 4:
Breakfast: Mango Smoothie Base & Greens
Lunch: Tuna Melt
Dinner: Loaded Bacon Mac & Cheese
Snack: Banana Oatmeal Cookies

Day 5:
Breakfast: 2-Ingredient Pancakes
Lunch: Pear & Banana Breakfast Salad
Dinner: Chicken Fried Rice
Snack: Apples & Dip
Day 6:
Breakfast: Mango Smoothie Base & Tofu
Lunch: Chicken Salad
Dinner: Cheesy Beef Egg Rolls
Snack: Banana Roll-Ups

Day 7:
Breakfast: Berry Monkey Bread Cinnamon Rolls
Lunch: Strawberry Sandwiches
Dinner: Air-Fried Parmesan Chicken
Snack: Baked Pumpkin Pie Egg Roll

Week 2: **Meal Prep Recipes for Kids**

Day 8:
Breakfast: Overnight Oats with Bananas & Walnuts
Lunch: Heirloom Tomato & Cucumber Toast
Dinner: Drumsticks with Apple Glaze
Snack: Pumpkin Cookies

Day 9:
Breakfast: Pineapple Oatmeal
Lunch: Baked Sweet Potatoes
Dinner: Lean Cheeseburgers
Snack: Chocolate Pudding

Day 10:
Breakfast: Cinnamon-Apple French Toast
Lunch: Leftover Turkey Noodle Soup
Dinner: Honey Grilled Chicken
Snack: Cranberry & Apple Dessert Risotto

Day 11:
Breakfast: Oatmeal & Blueberry Muffins
Lunch: Ravioli Lasagna
Dinner: Ground Pork Loaf
Snack: Applesauce

Day 12:
Breakfast: Cantaloupe Blueberry Breakfast Bowl
Lunch: Pizza Logs
Dinner: Lemon Chicken
Snack: Lemony Banana Mix

Day 13:
Breakfast: Cherries & Oats
Lunch: Turkey & Pear Pita Melt
Dinner: Pork Chops & Apples
Snack: Delicious Apple Pie

Day 14:
Breakfast: Tropical Breakfast Pie
Lunch: Baked Macaroni with Red Sauce
Dinner: BARBECUE Ranch Chicken Bites
Snack: Wacky Chocolate Cake

Chapter 6 Delicious Snacks – Dips & Spreads

- Black Bean Brownies – Vegan
- Breakfast Cookies
- Chocolate Biscotti
- Orange Cream Cheese Cookies & Nuts
- Peanut Butter Bites
- Tagalong Cookies Copycat Girl Scout ™Cookies
- 3 Ingredient Reese's Fudge

Movie Night Popcorn Galore
- Birthday Cake Popcorn
- Caramel Apple Popcorn
- Chocolate Coffee Peanut Butter Pretzel Popcorn
- Cool Ranch Popcorn
- Sriracha Popcorn

Dips & Spreads
- Baked Potato Dip
- Italian Basil Pesto – Vegan
- Jalapeno-Bacon & Corn-Cheese Dip
- Pea Guacamole with Tortilla Chips
- Spiced Smoky Red Pepper Dip

Made in the USA
San Bernardino, CA
22 February 2020